AF520956

'If you have ever thought the idea of self-love was vain or self-centred, this book will guide you to why self-love is vital for your emotional health, harmonious relationships, and living a fulfilled life. With numerous real-life stories of challenges resulting in positive change, you will be inspired for the possibilities for your life.'

**PATRICIA CRANE, PhD**

President & Co-Founder of Heart Inspired Presentations, Heal Your Life Trainer, Speaker, and Bestselling Author of *Ordering from The Cosmic Kitchen*

'Self-love is a rather underrated, in fact, often berated concept. Damini beautifully, and effectively illustrates the importance of using self-love as a tool for our betterment. This is a must-read book to change how we perceive our self-worth and to stop underselling ourselves.'

**KAVITA DEVGAN**

Nutrition & Wellness Consultant, Speaker, and Bestselling Author of *Fix It with Food*

'*Time to Come Home* is a special read. It is a book that finds a way to speak to you. It is relatable, real, and very personal. Books on self-love are usually centred on what self-love is all about, the idea, and the premise. Damini takes this a step further. While self-love is the primary subject, she brings forth so many concepts that one can practise to really bring about transformational change. The sections on inner-child work and changing your narrative resonate deeply. If self-love has been an area of trouble for you, this book is a must-read! The best part is, if you already practice self-love, this book will surprise you and show you how much deeper you can go. It is a journey, and it is for everyone!'

**SHASHANK GUPTA and SNEHA SHAH**

Founder Directors of ISRA and Transformational Coaches

'In the vast ocean of literary works, *Time to Come Home* by Damini Grover stands as a beacon of introspection and self-discovery. This book is not just a read; it is an experience. Grover delves deep into the universal struggle of self-worth, identity, and the quest for self-love. Through her poignant narrative, she captures the essence of what it means to feel lost in one's own life, a sentiment many of us can relate to but seldom voice.

The raw honesty with which she portrays the journey from self-doubt to self-acceptance is both heart-wrenching and inspiring. It is a reminder that amidst the chaos of external expectations, it is crucial to find our own voice, our own path, and most importantly, our own self. This book is a call to action for everyone who has ever felt disconnected from their true essence. It urges readers to embark on the most important journey they'll ever undertake—the journey inward. A must-read for anyone seeking authenticity and inner peace.'

**DIVYA PRAKASH DUBEY**
Author, Showrunner, and Dialogue Writer

'*Time to Come Home* is indeed a homecoming to some self-evident but often overlooked truths. She uses her own and the experiences of her clients to illustrate how moving towards self-love is a journey and not necessarily a destination. I love the guided self-reflection at the end of every chapter as she guides the reader to change the narrative about self and practice self-love and embrace their authentic self.'

**JAYNE MORRISON**
Regional Director at Six Seconds MEAI, Emotional Intelligence Master Trainer, Consultant, and Coach

'*Time to Come Home* serves as an exceptional compass for personal growth and fulfilment seekers. Organised into insightful sections, it offers practical exercises and prompts that facilitate introspection on one's beliefs, needs, and habits, empowering readers to set personal intentions. This book stands out by avoiding preachiness or judgment and refraining from dictating what readers should do. Instead, it encourages self-reflection, enabling individuals to make changes aligned with their unique path. In conclusion, I wholeheartedly endorse this book for anyone pursuing personal growth and fulfilment. It is a comprehensive guide featuring practical tools and exercises that foster self-awareness, self-love, and authenticity. Whether you are starting your self-discovery journey or seeking to deepen self-understanding, this resource will aid you in achieving your aspirations.

**NITIN SHAH**
Director at ICHARS

'*Time to Come Home* is a heartfelt exploration of self-love. Damini skilfully weaves together personal experiences, practical advice, and psychological insights to guide readers towards a journey of self-acceptance. It importantly explains the essential role of setting boundaries in nurturing one's well-being. The book delves into the profound connection between self-love and boundary setting within relationships, emphasising that these practices are integral to maintaining healthy connections. The author eloquently discusses the importance of recognising and honouring one's own needs and desires, showing readers how to communicate these without guilt or fear. Throughout the book, readers will find real-life narrations and actionable exercises that empower them to cultivate self-compassion and foster healthier, more fulfilling relationships.

It is a compassionate and empowering guide that gently reminds us that self-love is not a luxury but a fundamental necessity for leading a joyful and authentic life.'

**COLIN HALL**
Founder at Spa Wallah

'I found Damini's book to be the need of the hour. For years we have all struggled with self-love. Either we did not have the time, or the few people who did pay attention to the self were considered selfish and not self-loving. This book not only breaks that misconception but also gives us techniques that are easy to follow through. The case studies give an interesting insight and help reflect on our own behavioural traits. Damini's own narrative adds to a clinical perspective and gives depth to the issues. An absolute must!'

**SARIKA PANCHHI**
Founder and CEO of JiViSa Wellness

'*Time to Come Home* is a masterpiece on self-love. A subject which is widely talked about in the present time, yet so difficult to practice in real-life situations when we need it the most. Perhaps our deep-seated beliefs often make us think more about what we lack, rather than assuring us that we have within us all the resources to live a happy and satisfying life. What's needed is to shift our focus from 'looking outside' to seek validation, approval, and acceptance to 'looking within' and finding that we are 'enough' and worthy of our love, care, and respect.

In the book, Damini has explained the subject in depth and shared several case studies which I could easily relate to my own life, leading to some deep introspection and contemplation. I thoroughly gained from reading this book.'

**DEEPTI BATRA**
Founder Director of SharpKnol

'*Time to Come Home* is a journey to self-love. Damini with her deep insights, intellect and wisdom takes readers on a transformative path toward understanding their own worth. The book reminds us that practising self-care is not "selfish", but rather is essential for a fulfilling life. Through deeply personal anecdotes and practical advice, the book offers a roadmap for embracing self-compassion and one's authentic self.

The author's lucid writing style is both engaging and relatable, making the concepts simple to understand even for laypeople such as myself. Using psychological principles and spiritual insights, the book inspires readers to let go of self-doubt and embrace their inherent value. It stands out for its holistic approach to self-love, addressing the mental, emotional, and spiritual aspects of healing. It encourages readers to release the ghosts of the past and negative self-talk. This book is essential reading for you if you are seeking to embark on a transformative journey to "discover, love and embrace your true self.'

**NIKHIL KAPUR**
Founder, Transformative Wellness

'Start your journey to self-love today. Get your copy of *Time to Come Home* by Damini and embark on a path to a more confident, joyful you. Through personal anecdotes and expert advice, this book reveals the secrets to building a strong foundation of self-love. This is yet again a very sound book which is very encouraging to the reader in a discovery which is inwards.'

**MOHIT GUPTA**
Co-Founder, FROB (City Book Leaders)

'Damini's book provides a refreshing guide to the self-love vs selfishness dilemma, offering clarity by addressing common misconceptions. Its practical approach, with self-reflection exercises in each chapter, bridges theory and action, enabling tangible personal growth. In contrast to idealised portrayals on social media, this book offers a logical and balanced perspective on self-love, making it a valuable resource for those seeking genuine self-acceptance and love.'

**SNEHI SINGH**
Co-Founder, JiViSa Wellness

'Self-love is a journey and only some can find it on their own. For the other lost souls, who feel that something is missing in their lives, Damini holds your hand and takes you through the beautiful process of finding yourself and loving yourself so that others can love you the way you want them to. This book is a must-pick up for everyone in today's age where there is so much self-doubt and anxiety around the same.'

RACHNA CHHACHHI
Co-Founder, RachnaRestores, Author, Fertility & Nutrition Expert, and Mental Health Therapist

'Some time ago, I saw a movie in which the lead actor announces that she is her own favourite! How powerful that statement was and how I wished more people experienced this emotion of self-love! Being a trainer in the space of self-development, I often come across people who need to meet themselves to uncover their blind spots and walk with themselves to start living a fuller life. *Time to Come Home* by Damini Grover is a complete guide; that invisible helping hand to help readers understand themselves. It not only helps to uncover the blind spots but also walk those miles by taking baby steps. The backdrop of real-life stories helps you to relate and understand yourself better. Through this book, the author provides a great reminder to be gentle with oneself. It lends that much-needed unseen hand to hold, to come out and be a happier version of their selves. This book is your perfect companion on your journey of self-love.'

DR RANJANA MITTAL
Additional General Manager and Corporate Trainer at NTPC

'Writing and dancing are how Damini expresses herself, and since this book comes from her, I can confidently say that it comes from her heart. The structure and topics covered are relevant to each one of us, and coupled with the conversations she has included, *Time to Come Home* is a perfect companion for everyone on a journey of self-discovery and love. She has turned it into a whole package by not only describing each aspect of self-love but also by including the barriers that stop us from loving ourselves wholly. A must-read.'

**MALLIKA BHATIA**
Psychotherapist, Hypnotherapist, Trainer, and Founder at Swayam

'The book beautifully delves into the complex realm of self-love, drawing parallels between the luxury of high-end items and the perceived luxury of self-love. Damini adeptly captures the struggle many individuals face in embracing self-love, portraying it as a concept that feels distant and unattainable for many. The comparison between self-love and selfishness is particularly poignant, highlighting a common misconception that often inhibits individuals from fully embracing self-love. The narrative skilfully navigates through various aspects of self-love, including its impact on personal fulfilment, relationships, and professional endeavours.

Moreover, the author's personal journey and professional experience as a counselling psychologist and Heal Your Life Coach lend authenticity and depth to the narrative. By sharing insights gained from working with individuals struggling with self-love, the author adds credibility to their message while offering hope and practical guidance to readers. The call to action embedded in the conclusion encourages readers to embark on a journey toward self-love, framing it as a transformative process that starts from within and radiates outward. Overall, this piece serves as an insightful exploration of self-love, offering valuable reflections and guidance for those seeking to cultivate a deeper sense of self-acceptance and love.'

**JOYDEV CHATTERJEE**
Hypnotherapist, Tarot Card Reader, and Founder at Celestial Corner

# Time to Come Home

## Sowing the Seeds *of* Self-Love *for* Lasting Happiness

Damini Grover

HAY HOUSE

HAY HOUSE INDIA

New Delhi • London • Sydney

Carlsbad, California • New York City

**Hay House Publishers (India) Pvt Ltd**
Muskaan Complex, Plot No. 3, B-2, Vasant Kunj, New Delhi – 110070, India

Hay House LLC, P.O. Box 5100, Carlsbad, CA 92018-5100, USA
Hay House UK Ltd, The Sixth Floor, Watson House, 54 Baker Street, London W1U 7BU, UK
Hay House Australia Publishing Pty Ltd, 18/36 Ralph St., Alexandria NSW 2015, Australia

Email: contact@hayhouse.co.in
Website: www.hayhouse.co.in



First published by Hay House India, 2024
10 9 8 7 6 5 4 3 2 1

ISBN 978-81-97222-85-6
ISBN 978-81-97222-84-9 (Ebook)

Printed at Replika Press Pvt Ltd

FSC
www.fsc.org
MIX
Paper | Supporting responsible forestry
FSC™ C016779

Hay House is committed to a sustainable future for our business, our readers and our planet. This book is made from Forest Stewardship Council® certified paper.

This book is dedicated to my family, Joy Sir, Mallika, and everyone who has ever been connected to me. You have made me who I am today.

This book is especially dedicated to my inner child who struggled, fought, got hurt, and made mistakes but emerged stronger each day.

# Contents


Foreword 15

Author's Note 18

**1. Discovering Self-Love 19**

1.1 What Is Self-Love? 21

1.2 The Anatomy of Self-Love 27

1.3 Why Self-Love? 41

**2. Barriers to Self-Love 47**

2.1 Misconceptions about Self-Love 49

2.2 Unblocking Self-Love: Overcoming Limiting Habits and Behaviours 55

2.3 Hidden Blocks to Self-Love 75

**3. Uncovering the Hidden Blocks to Self-Love 77**

3.1 Twisted Ways of the Mind 79

3.2 Say Hello to Your Mind 85

3.3 Digging Deeper 89

3.4 Understanding the Origin of Beliefs 97

3.5 Unravelling the Sources and Influences that Shape Beliefs 101

**4. Finding Love within and Changing the Narrative 111**

4.1 Harnessing Awareness 113

4.2 Understanding the Narrative 121

4.3 Acknowledging Resistance 127

| | | |
|---|---|---|
| **5.** | **The Power of Changing Your Narrative** | **133** |
| 5.1 | Stories of Self-Love | 135 |
| **6.** | **Cultivating Self-Love** | **141** |
| 6.1 | Nurturing Childhood Gaps | 143 |
| 6.2 | Opening the Doors to Your Inner Child | 161 |
| **7.** | **Transcending the 'I Am Unworthy' Narrative** | **173** |
| 7.1 | Embracing Transformation: From Resistance to Change | 175 |
| **8.** | **Embracing Gratitude and Forgiveness** | **239** |
| 8.1 | The Transformative Power of Forgiveness | 241 |
| 8.2 | Forgiving Yourself | 249 |
| 8.3 | The Gift of Gratefulness | 253 |
| **9.** | **Coming Home to Your Authentic Self** | **259** |
| 9.1 | The Art of Authenticity | 261 |
| **10.** | **Onward Bound: The Journey Continues** | **267** |
| 10.1 | Harnessing Your Inner Coach and Cheerleader | 269 |
| Acknowledgements | | 279 |

# Foreword

When I finished reading this book, there was an odd echo of Leo Tolstoy's famous sentence from *Anna Karenina* in my head. I heard: 'All happy families are alike; each unhappy family is unhappy in its own way.' As all happy individuals are alike; each unhappy individual is unhappy in his own way.

Recipes of happiness have been served to us since early civilisation, sometimes in the form of proverbs and phrases, and sometimes through parables and fables. Yet the modern mind calls these words of wisdom truisms or simplistic. But when one searches for meaningful answers in science, religion, philosophy, or psychology, the already tired and heavy mind tends to get bamboozled by what it perceives as jargon. This book by Damini Grover is, therefore, an exception and a relief as complex ideas have been conveyed clearly and understandably without being simplistic.

*Time to Come Home* is a must-read for someone who feels unhappy with themselves and, as a result, with others. I have always held a simplistic thought that I am truly able to love others, be empathetic and show kindness towards them because I nurture those same feelings towards myself as well. That belief of mine finds a great resonance here. Yet this book is not a quick fix or a magic formula for self-love. Nor is it a long and boring lecture from a perfectionist, teaching you about perfectionism and the easy way to achieve 'perfect' happiness. In fact, both the ideas of perfectionism and happiness are explored in a loving and thoughtful manner.

Damini has delved deep into her own previously perceived imperfect life, making it easy for others to identify with her. She comes across not as a preacher, but as a calm and wise friend shaped by experience. Engaging in conversations with real-life clients who have found their lives imperfect, Damini offers a colourful bouquet of warm ideas. Through their prism, she encourages us to embrace our lives with greater acceptance while also finding the strength to make necessary improvements for a better life.

The most interesting thing about this book is that she is not going to play it alone, playing alone is no fun after all. With the help of simple exercises, which I am sure you will love and understand, you will also be a part of the discovery of self-love. It clearly establishes the idea that your behaviour towards others is often a reflection of your relationship with yourself.

She is, however, clear that acceptance of yourself does not mean denial or excuses to not improve certain areas. This book is also honest enough to emphasise that the road is going to be long and, like most things, it will not be easy either. Based on her own experience, she is certain that living a better life, happier, and healthier life is not impossible. This book offers hope that by following some key basic principles, you can live a fulfilled life.

It is, of course, a possibility that you will find love from or with others. However, what happens if you do not find it? *Time to Come Home* provides reasonable and effective answers to this question. It clears the most common misconceptions about self-love effectively, clearly, and with logic and credible instances.

In this book, Damini has clearly established the importance of the recipe of self-love. She also mentions some home-grown ingredients of real-life experience and examples. With simple questions, she will guide you through the cooking of what I believe is a fantastic meal of ideas promoting health and happiness, to be savoured slowly. There book avoids unnecessary theory that might confuse you. Laced with some wonderful quotes from people in all walks of life, she will show you why it is important for us to heal and be imperfect if not perfectly happy.

With an acceptance of others and a clear admission of her own fallibilities, the author deeply reminds us that we are not alone in our struggles. It does not have to be this way forever. Together, we can embark on a journey towards a life of better understanding, self-love, and self-care. Therefore, it is truly time to come home with this book.

**—RITESH SHAH**

Screenplay & Dialogue Writer, Hindi Film Industry

# Author's Note

Before flipping open this book, you must have had certain expectations from it—to guide you, support you, motivate you, talk to your inner child, or, perhaps, you were simply enticed by the title. Whatever the expectation may be, at the core, you are interested to know about self-love, seeking clarity and guidance about approaching your life with tenderness, care, and love.

I, too, have also struggled to comprehend and embrace the concept of self-love for a long time. Through countless personal and professional experiences, I have come to understand that our notions about love and self-love are flawed, and it is about time we correct them. It is only after falling prey to several misleading ideas about self-love that I now realise we can have meaningful experiences and relationships only when we look inwards and listen to the voice of love that is trying to guide us. However, we are unable to tune into it for various reasons.

I have written this book to help you understand the hurdles that may be blocking your path to self-love. I hope that the exercises within will help you reflect, bringing about a positive shift within yourself.

Let this book be a companion on your journey to loving yourself more each day. After all, you deserve your own love.

# 1
# DISCOVERING SELF-LOVE

*'Self-love is the source of all our other loves.'*
**—Pierre Corneille**

## 1.1

## What Is Self-Love?

Before I go on about self-love, let us start with an activity that will help you understand self-love.

Step 1: Think of all the people you love—your parents, siblings, partner(s), friends, pets, etc.

Step 2: Think of how you show your love to them. List them mentally or on paper. You'll probably write things along the lines of:

- Give them time
- Take care of them
- Feel saddened, hurt, or affected by their pain
- Listen to them
- Solve their problems
- Support them
- Encourage and motivate them
- Uplift them when they are feeling down
- Shower them with presents
- Go out together
- Appreciate them
- Celebrate their achievements
- Compliment them
- Understand and let go of their mistakes
- Forgive them
- Tell them 'I Love You'

There can be endless unique ways to show love to people. Going by these acts, it is only fair to say that to love someone is to do things to make them feel loved. As a manner of doing things, we *give* them our time, presence, energy, acceptance, understanding, support, compassion, and kindness. Therefore, we can say that love is an act of 'giving'.

At least, for me it is. I look at love as an emotion with an action component attached to it. Love is an extremely powerful human emotion that encapsulates several other emotions that, when acted upon, give meaning and direction to those who come under its purview. As an emotion, love makes you want to reach out to, take care of, understand, provide comfort, and nurture someone. In essence, love is a collection of emotions and actions that we show towards something or someone.

*To love someone or something is to treat them with warmth, understanding, acceptance, care, and concern for their well-being. Genuine love is not about taking things but giving them what you have.*

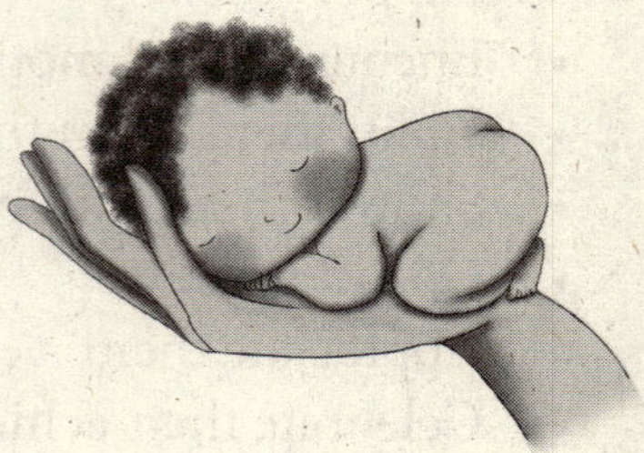

When a baby is born, it needs emotional, psychological, and physical nourishment from its caregivers, especially the mother. It gradually starts to flourish and grow with the help of this love. Similarly, when you plant a seed, you need to give it the right amount of sunshine, water, and manure consistently to make sure it blooms into a beautiful flower or tree.

Genuine, whole-hearted love is about taking care of others and providing them with what they need to bloom. It is all about nurturing and nourishment. If we do this for others, then why cannot we do so for ourselves? What is wrong about giving ourselves some acceptance, care, attention, and warmth? Love is love, whether you give it to yourself or someone else, there is nothing wrong or catastrophic about it. It is a beautiful, empowering emotion that can nurture, heal, and transform us as well as others into the best version possible.

Unfortunately, we have distorted the definition of love to suit our own needs. Perpetuating the 'self-love is selfish' culture ensures people do not connect with their true selves and follow societal notions. It makes life easier if everyone simply does what is expected of them without any retaliation or opposition. By asking for conformity, we kill everyone's individuality.

Self-love is a transformative mindset, a profound way of relating to oneself that unlocks our unique potential, fosters healthy growth, and enriches our mental, emotional, and physical well-being. Without embracing this mindset, we remain tethered to a life of disconnection. It becomes a superficial existence, where we seek love solely from external sources, hoping and relying on them to fulfil our deepest needs. While this approach may suffice if we receive some measure of love externally, it becomes problematic when the external supply dwindles or ceases altogether. Suddenly, we find ourselves adrift, without a source to replenish our love and nourish our souls.

I once conducted a training session where one of the participants shared with the group that he often felt guilty if he did something for himself. He either could not take a stand for himself and when he did, he was gaslit into believing that he was the problem. He felt worthless. I am sure a lot of us can relate to this. We think that love is only about giving yourself to another person, thinking they are responsible for meeting our needs and making us feel loved. Thus, we do things the way they want us to, get some kind of reward from them, and the cycle continues. However, the minute there is no reward, we have nothing to fall back on.

This is where self-love comes in. Your love for yourself allows you to give yourself the due consideration that you deserve by being human. It grants you the ability to honour your strengths, accept yourself, and approach your weaknesses with compassion. When you genuinely love yourself, you liberate yourself from the entanglements and burdens imposed by the world or even by yourself. These are the very strings that inflict pain and hinder your growth at each level. It is as vital as nourishing food and water. Just as consuming the right kind of food at the right time and in the right amount sustains your physical health, self-love provides a stable foundation for your overall well-being. Without sufficient self-love, you will lack the stability necessary to navigate life's challenges.

Look at the world around you, and you will find people who tell you how they spent their entire lives doing things for others, ignoring their own needs and wishes, and remain unhappy. They feel as if they do not matter. If you ask them what they do for themselves, some will say nothing while others will ponder for a long time. This sense of being unhappy, unimportant, and non-existent is a direct manifestation of a lack of self-love. Perhaps, if they had paid attention to their needs and desires then their life would have been different.

In essence, loving yourself is about giving yourself the time, attention, care, respect, understanding, compassion, kindness, and forgiveness that you deserve just like you would give to those you love.

When I asked Parul what brought her to her first therapy session, she said, 'I don't know.'

After probing a little, she went on to say, 'I don't know what's going on in my life. I feel as if I am on a never-ending and twisting roller-coaster ride, and I just cannot seem to get off it. I wake up feeling wired and anxious. All I can think of are the things I need to get done during the day, but when I sit down to work, my mind goes blank. This has been going on for months now! I am not able to sleep or slow down. I cannot say no to anyone so I keep piling on more and more work and now I just cannot seem to handle anything! I don't know how I reached here, but I cannot seem to find my way back. Can you help?'

Even as she was speaking, I could see that she was extremely anxious.

I asked her, 'Parul, right at this moment, what do you think you need? What could help you to ease out a bit?'

She thought for some time, smiled, and said, 'I do need to ease out, don't I?' Her anger and frustration were obvious as she continued to speak.

'I need to get off this rollercoaster! I want to step down and pay some attention to myself. I am looking after everything and everyone but me, and I am tired of it!'

There it was—the lack of love for herself . . . hanging in the air.

As we continued with our conversation, Parul gradually became aware of several other ways she was not giving herself enough of what she needed. She realised that she needed to make tremendous changes in her life and the way she was relating to herself; so that she could feel more at ease, content and fulfilled.

Eventually, her journey was about finding her ways to love herself. Just like it is for all of us.

# 1.2
# The Anatomy of Self-Love

The other day I decided to cook pasta. Since I did not know the process, I searched for it on the internet, acquired and assembled all the ingredients, and got to work. Once the pasta was ready, I tasted it and realised that it had not come out well. The spaghetti was not boiled properly, the sauce was undercooked, and the spices were all wrong! Of course, I was disappointed. But I did not spend the whole day mulling over it. I went over what needed to be fixed and cooked it again. This time it turned out pretty good!

Learning how to love yourself is like cooking pasta—or whatever you wish to cook. You need to know all the ingredients, add the right kind of spices, and allow enough time to cook properly. Sometimes you will get it right, while other times you may not. But what matters is that you keep at it.

Loving yourself requires a whole blend of ingredients. Let us understand them in more detail.

**Ingredient #1: Self-Awareness**

Self-awareness is about knowing yourself, which warrants an insight into:

- Your thoughts, emotional responses and reactions, and behaviours you engage in

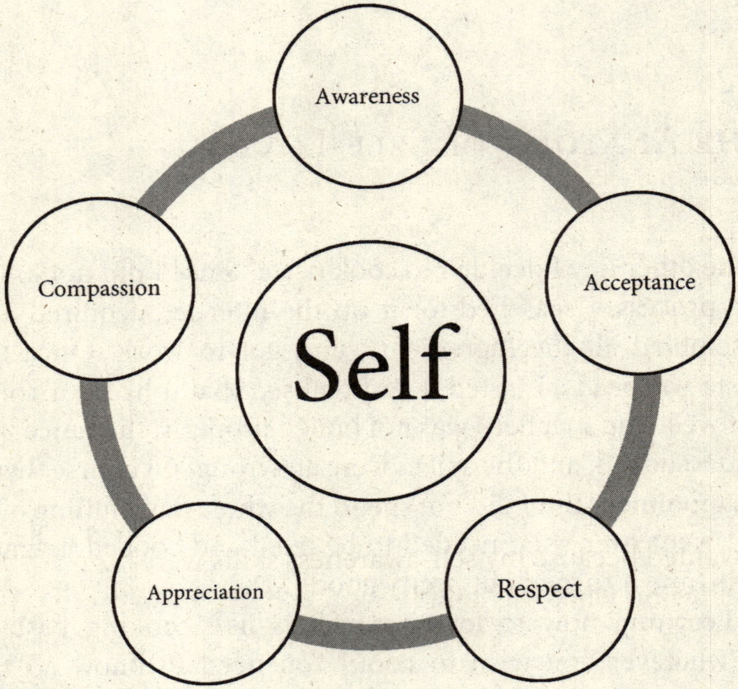


- The impact of your responses and actions on people and the environment around you
- The impact others have on you

Self-awareness extends far beyond knowledge of your food choices, fashion preferences, or colour preferences. It goes deeper and is an ongoing process. It involves understanding and being conscious of how your experiences have shaped you into a unique individual. It involves being aware of your strengths and weaknesses and recognising the areas of life that demand your attention and the ones you are content with. Self-awareness encompasses the knowledge of ourselves, our functioning, and the factors that contribute to identity and values, we constantly play catch-up, struggling to comprehend the events and experiences that unfold before us. While self-awareness might seem like a basic inherent quality, it is astonishing how many individuals lack this profound insight into their being and what shapes their essence.

Over the years I have interacted and worked with individuals who had no idea who they were or what they wanted from life. Some were not even aware of their favourite colour or the kind of food they preferred. They simply adopted what was dictated to them or what was socially appropriate.

I was one of them, too. Growing up, I was oblivious to what I wanted because my self-awareness skills were non-existent. Following what was told became a habit and nothing more was expected of me. I also found shelter in following others rather than carving my path. Then, in a eureka moment, I realised that I would never be able to move forward unless I started paying attention to myself. I knew I had to know myself to truly love myself. Everything did not pan out all at once, as initially, I understood what did not work for me. After multiple trials and errors, I figured out what I liked. It enabled me to discern my true needs and desires, eventually leading me towards clarity and understanding.

By directing your focus towards your thoughts, emotions, actions, and underlying motivations, you enhance your ability to actively participate in your journey. It goes much beyond just day-to-day awareness of what's going on in your mind and body. It is the ability to dig deeper and find all those other layers that make you who you are. It is about knowing how your life circumstances have contributed to your personality, behaviours, and overall outlook. Thus, self-awareness is the first step towards self-love.

Till the time we are alive, we will continue to discover facets of our personality and behaviours. If we fail to take control, someone else will. None of us want that and it is this muscle of self-awareness that helps us to make the necessary choices in life.

So, how do you become self-aware? By paying attention to yourself with openness and curiosity.

**Ingredient #2: Self-Acceptance**

You cannot cook pasta with ramen noodles, can you? Similarly, you cannot love yourself without accepting your true form. Pasta looks and tastes a certain way and the same goes for noodles. You cannot mix your personality with the ideas of other people. All of it has to be in sync with your particular attributes.

Acceptance means *'It is what it is'* without any judgment, criticism, blame, or resentment. To accept something means to no longer struggle to make it different, i.e., not wishing for a pen to look like a phone. A pen looks and feels a certain way and you cannot change it; however, your attitude, likes, and dislikes towards it are a different story.

Self-acceptance involves being at peace with how you look, what your skills and abilities are, your talents and strengths, and your awareness of the areas you need to improve. It is to manifest *'I am okay with the way I am'*. We are all born with certain attributes, characteristics, aptitudes, and interest areas. We need to understand our unique approach to the world and our choice to not copy others. After all, the world is no fun if we are all clones of each other!

Acceptance does not mean complacency or resignation to the fact that 'I am doomed to be this way!' It does not support being ignorant of our mistakes and giving excuses like, 'I am how I am. Deal with it!' Responsibility is crucial to self-acceptance. You must respect every part of yourself and work to change without tearing yourself apart. If there are certain attributes that we would like to change, we at least need to acknowledge their existence with respect.

*In the words of Nathaniel Branden, 'Self-acceptance is my refusal to be in an adversarial relationship with myself.'*

*Acceptance for self, people, and situations simply means 'it is what it is'. This is what it looks like, feels like, and behaves like without constantly beating yourself or others for it.*

Support your uniqueness by cultivating a sense of genuine appreciation for your true self and embracing your individuality. Then, with respect and kindness, pursue opportunities for personal growth and make deliberate changes that contribute to your journey of self-improvement.

**Ingredient #3: Self-Respect**

During one of my candid conversations with my father during high school, he said, 'You shouldn't demand respect, but command it.'

While I was too young to make sense of his words, this piece of wisdom has stayed with me.

Think of all the people you admire and respect. Notice that your respect for them stems from who they are, not because of some predisposed societal idea of them. They not only show regard for others but also ensure they do not compromise themselves in the process. The truth is if you do not respect yourself—give due consideration to your needs and choices—then the world around you will not either. When you make yourself excessively available, compromise your goals, and tolerate inappropriate behaviour, you inadvertently invite more of the same into your life. Despite receiving respect from others on occasion, you may struggle to fully embrace and acknowledge it.

Respecting yourself entails maintaining your dignity, advocating for what feels right, honouring your choices, expressing your discomfort, and refusing to settle for mistreatment.

✿

I asked Anu as we began to explore her reasons for coming to therapy.

Me: 'What brings you here?'

Anu: 'I have been keeping unwell for the past few months. The other day I visited a doctor, and he told me that I seemed to be under a lot of stress and should seek some counselling or therapy. I couldn't understand much of what he said but I decided to book a session anyway. So here I am.'

Me: 'All right. Could you tell me more about what's happening with you lately?'

Anu: 'I feel tired all the time. I struggle to wake up early and somehow manage to send my children to school. After my husband leaves for the office, I aimlessly sit around and do nothing. Sometimes the whole day goes by, and I realise I haven't even showered. I don't have much of an appetite, so I end up skipping meals. I have also started losing my cool at pretty much everything. I mostly keep to myself, rarely stepping outside or talking to anyone. There have also been occurrences of midnight anxiety attacks.'

Me: 'How long has this been going on?'

Anu (upon careful reflection): 'It's been quite a while, I believe. I have somehow managed myself till now, but I don't think I can anymore. There's also a constant unexplainable anger within me.'

Me: 'Who are you angry at?'

Anu: 'Everyone! My husband, in-laws, children, parents, friends. I don't want to talk to anyone. They all make me so mad!'

Me: 'What do they do that makes you so mad?'

Anu (her anger and frustration mounting): 'They don't care about me! They don't respect me at all. When I am doing things their way, it's fine. But the moment I want to do something on my own or for myself, everyone has issues. I am okay with adjusting; I have been doing it for years. But the worst is the disrespect that comes with it. Those nasty comments, snide remarks—they make me so mad, and I just cannot seem to take a stand for myself. So, I mostly just give in to prevent exploding with anger. Yet, no one considers how I feel because to them I am just throwing a tantrum.'

Me: 'That must be difficult. I can see that you are in a lot of pain.'

Anu sat there quietly for a few minutes and then continued.

Anu: 'I have dealt with a lot of nonsense over the years, and I don't think I can handle it anymore. But I also don't know where to start.'

Me: 'I understand it's hard for you to change your behaviour and ways of handling things overnight. But the fact that you are here tells me that you are ready to change. So, to begin with, if you could change one thing in the next few weeks, what would it be?'

Anu: 'I would like to treat myself with a little more respect. Rather, I need to *learn* to do that. When unsavoury things are said to me or unfair restrictions are being imposed, I want to stand my ground without backing down. Usually, I spend hours crying in my room and questioning why I didn't say anything whenever something like this happens.'

Me: 'And what would change for you when you do start respecting yourself?'

Anu: 'Well, I guess, I won't feel as caged and suffocated as I do now. I know I have allowed things to happen, and I could have done certain things differently. I will be able to take better care of myself and do the things that I want to if people around me have a problem with it. I want to join a dance or yoga class, travel with friends, spend money on myself, and just be free. I know people around me won't understand a lot of things, and that's fine by me. Most importantly, when someone misbehaves with me, I want to tell them to stop!'

Me: 'Well, that sounds empowering. So, how about we explore ways to make this happen for you?'

Anu: 'Can it happen?'

Me: 'Yes. It will take some time and effort. But it will certainly happen.'

Anu was sitting with a slight smile at the corner of her mouth. From walking in with sadness in her eyes to uncovering the deep-seated anger, frustration, and resentment, she had, now moved to a place of hope.

After a month of therapy sessions, she walked in proudly one day. I asked her what had happened, when she boldly announced, 'I took a stand for myself this week!'

Me: 'Okay, that sounds amazing! Tell me more.'

Anu: 'My husband and I were in the middle of an everyday argument when he started making personal comments that were unrelated to the topic. He raised his voice to an uncomfortable decibel. Initially, I paid no heed to it, but after some time, I took a deep breath, gathered myself, and said to him: "Look, we can maturely talk about the issue only if you talk to me properly." Although I said it as coolly as possible, he responded with a hurt ego: "No, I will not. I will talk the way I want to!" That's when I said: "Fine then. I refuse to be part of this conversation because I will not be spoken to like this. We can talk later when you are a bit calm," and walked away.'

Me: 'How did that feel?'

Anu: 'It was empowering. I didn't give in, I didn't tolerate, or start shouting back. I stood my ground and respected myself. I feel quite proud of myself.'

Before we expect anyone to respect us, we need to respect ourselves. How you carry yourself, speak about yourself, and engage with other people is a strong determinant of how others are likely to engage with you.

However, people often confuse self-respect with ego. The ego always stems from insecurity about who we are. The ego is instant and reactive. It does not consider the other person. It is all about I, me, and myself. The voice of ego tells you to be stern and stubborn, disagree with anything that does not satisfy you, and stick to your stand regardless of the circumstances. It is often responsible for damaging relationships. Self-respect, on the other hand, is rooted in security with oneself—it is responsive. When you respect yourself, you do not settle for any kind of mistreatment. Hence, embracing self-love entails acknowledging your worth and refusing to treat yourself as a secondary choice because you know you deserve more.

**Ingredient #4: Self-Appreciation**

Question yourself: When you achieve something, do you compliment yourself, admire your creation, or pat yourself on the back? Or do you simply toss it away and wait for someone else to praise you only to disregard it or attribute it to luck? If you do the latter, you are depriving yourself of self-love.

Appreciating yourself does not mean boasting or gloating. Instead, it's about:

- Giving due consideration to your hard work, struggles, strengths, and achievements
- Knowing and believing in the inherent value of your place in the world
- Enjoying who you are and what you can create

A few years ago, when Facebook was the IT social media platform, I took an interest in it and became quite active. Once, I clicked a selfie that I liked a lot and posted it. Instantly, I liked it before anyone else. Someone commented under that photograph, 'LOL, who likes their pic? That's so lame!' and I wondered what was so wrong in liking my own picture. After all, it's mine. I clicked it. I like it.

And this my friend, is what appreciating yourself looks like. You have a basic liking for who you are and all the work that you put in, irrespective of the results. Even on difficult days, you are at least able to tell yourself, *I tried my best!*

In the absence of this capacity to recognise and cherish your worth, you will incessantly pursue validation, approval, and appreciation from others. While it is natural to desire positive feedback from those around us, relying solely on their words and opinions as the foundation for self-value can be detrimental to us. What if they do not share that perspective? What if they dislike what you have done and all that you have achieved? What then?

Subsequently, it becomes essential to establish a firm foundation for yourself where you genuinely appreciate your accomplishments, regardless of external validation.

Aisha: 'You know, I have noticed that I do this quite often and was wondering if it's normal.'

Me: 'What are you talking about? Can you help me understand?'

Aisha: 'I have noticed that every time I achieve something or do something good, I feel the need to get someone's approval. I wonder if this is normal.'

Me: 'Could you elaborate on "getting it approved by someone"?'

Aisha: 'For instance, I was supposed to give a presentation at work the other day. I worked hard on it and did a good job. But until I had shown the presentation to 5–6 people, I didn't feel confident enough to present it, and post-presentation, I lingered around to ask people for feedback. The entire team appreciated my presentation, but it didn't feel enough.'

Me: 'Hmm . . . I have a question.'

Aisha: 'Sure.'

Me: 'Are you able to appreciate your effort, hard work and what you have created or done at the end of the day? Do you ever compliment yourself that you have done a good job?'

Aisha: 'Umm . . . No. I don't even think I have done a good job most of the time!'

Me: 'Why's that?'

Aisha (looking down): 'Because I never think that what I do or how I do things matters. For me, it's always been about keeping others around me satisfied, making their opinions trump mine. Maybe that's why I am always on the edge about what people say or think about me.'

Me: 'It must be exhausting to constantly consider others' opinions.'

Aisha: 'Yeah, it is. Maybe if I had learnt to appreciate myself more then I wouldn't be so worried about what others think of me or my work, right?'

Me (smiling): 'Yes, then you wouldn't have to run after validation all the time.'

This ability to look at your efforts, contributions, and progress—no matter how small—is crucial as it acknowledges your journey and directs you towards your goal. If we also fail to recognise and value our worth, we risk living a life devoid of meaning and purpose. Thus, cultivating the ability to recognise the positive impact we bring into our lives, and of others, is an essential component of self-love.

**Ingredient #5: Self-Compassion**

Being compassionate is to show care, concern, empathy, and kindness towards others. When someone is suffering, you can understand and feel their pain and are willing to extend a helping hand. Showing such kindness is a basic human trait. After all, we all need each other's support.

Having compassion for ourselves is no different. It is essential for our survival and growth. Human beings are fallible, bound to make mistakes, and constantly face challenges. Therefore, we need to be able to extend this compassionate hand to ourselves as well.

Being kind to someone makes us feel good, making the other person feel seen, heard, validated, and supported. It creates a good vibe. Self-compassion is turning this supportive and empathetic energy towards the self into a warm embrace. Such compassion gives us the strength to turn setbacks into opportunities for learning and growth. It replaces the feelings of misery, self-pity, and hopelessness with space for sanguine thoughts. However, a lot of us believe that self-compassion is akin to self-pity and it's all about indulging in oneself. It does not involve making excuses for your mistakes or behaving like a victim and feeling sorry for yourself all the time.

Self-compassion is cutting yourself some slack along with taking personal responsibility for what's happening in your life, especially the things you are struggling with. Instead of coming at yourself with an immensely self-critical and judgemental voice, you should say, *I know it's hard for me, but I did the best I could, and I need to learn from it.* No matter what anyone says, always trust your voice the most.

Dr Kristin Neff, in her pioneering research on self-compassion, has shown that being self-compassionate has great benefits for our psychological well-being because it is associated with greater emotional resilience, more accurate self-concepts, more caring behaviour, and less reactive anger. According to Neff, 'We cannot always get what we want. We cannot always be who we want to be. When this reality is denied or resisted, suffering arises in the form of stress, frustration, and self-criticism. When this reality is accepted with benevolence, however, we generate positive emotions of kindness and care that help us cope.'

Extending a kind and compassionate hand to ourselves shows that we are on our team. When life gets tough or when we are gripped by moments of inadequacy, we can tune into this soft, caring, warm voice that's able to pull us out of our darkness and show us the way forward. In fine, it is about learning to be your own best friend and having your own back.

## 1.3
## Why Self-Love?

When Rashmi walked into my clinic for her first session, she looked extremely worn out. A young woman in her mid-thirties and mother to a wonderful daughter, she was on her last legs. A pretty woman who never cared much about her appearance looked hopeless. She was lost, confused, and disappointed.

When I asked her what brought her to this session, she said, 'I don't know. I feel something is wrong with me, but I am unable to put a name to it. I don't feel like myself at all. I no longer recognise myself.'

'Who do you think you have become?' I inquired.

'I have become this person who's never happy. I am always grumpy and irritated, constantly lashing out at everyone around me, something I never did before. I had a sweet relationship with my 8-year-old daughter, but I am messing that up as well. I have lost my patience around her, and I feel terrible,' she relayed.

I probed a little more to ask about her relationship with the other members of her family, which instantly opened Pandora's Box. She informed me that while her relationship with other family members has been great thus far, it is her relationship with her husband that she cannot seem to figure out. Their marriage was arranged by the elders of their respective families, and with mutual feelings, they decided to be together. Everything was fine in the beginning as they spent quality time together—going out and having fun—but eventually, things began to change.

To be a good wife and daughter-in-law, she focused all her attention on her family and married life. She gave up her desire to work and be independent. She structured her life around her husband and dismissed her needs and desires. She would always do whatever he asked of her despite her discomfort. Her husband would often disregard her sacrifices and efforts, if taking care of the house was her job. He wouldn't give her money for her expenses, reasoning that it was not required, and she could do without the things she wanted.

She accepted everything without questioning, arguing, or retaliating. Gradually, her hurt reached its limit and transformed into anger and resentment towards her ungrateful husband—she was like a live volcano erupting on everyone and unable to help herself.

During our work together, we uncovered the fact that she was not getting the love, appreciation, or validation she needed because she never learnt to give it to herself.

In her attempt to be the 'good wife', 'good daughter-in-law', and 'good mother', she had stopped nurturing herself with the ideal of selflessness. Unfortunately, that's not how it played out for her.

If we cannot provide ourselves with love by nourishing our self-awareness, acceptance, respect, and compassion, we may not always receive it from external sources either. In such situations, we must rely on ourselves to take the required actions and avoid becoming passive recipients of whatever is being offered to us.

Siya was a bright young girl who was superbly talented at everything she did. Even on the days filled with self-doubt, someone would always show up and tell her how amazing she was. However, she could never absorb the praise because she was too busy criticising herself over the smallest of mistakes, being harsh towards herself. She could never believe all the appreciation and encouragement she received until she woke up to the fact that her relationship with herself needed to change. It needed to become gentle and loving.

Such innumerable anecdotes are available where people are operating from this extreme lack of self-love and wonder why they are not happy. Perhaps, you find it relatable, too. When you operate from a space of acceptance, respect, and compassion for yourself, the following things begin to happen:

a. Your mental, emotional, and physical health improve. Think of yourself as a plant. Just like a plant needs certain things for its survival, so do you. When you focus on your mental, emotional, physical, and spiritual needs, you can take the necessary steps to meet them.
b. You become self-reliant because you understand that, as you are an adult, no one else is accountable for your needs. You are responsible for choosing the right kind of people, opportunities, and relationships that can

nurture you. You will feel sad, dejected, hurt, angry, and heartbroken if someone cannot give you what you want or need, but you will be able to support yourself by taking the necessary steps and making decisions to support your well-being.

c. You become better at decision-making.
d. You can take necessary risks that aid your growth instead of being stuck in your comfort zone.
e. You declutter and filter out tasks, people, relationships, and events that do not serve you anymore. You value your time, energy, and effort and direct them better.
f. You stop taking things personally because you are secure with yourself. A random comment on your body, looks, work, and behaviour wouldn't pull you down.
g. You become more loving and giving towards those you care about because you understand that there is no competition in relationships. It is about adjusting your efforts to suit the needs of the hour.
h. You begin to enjoy being yourself and want to explore and learn more about yourself and the world around you.
i. You set healthy boundaries because you know you matter.
j. You are at ease with your true self and not some half-baked version of yourself.

The struggle to practice self-love despite its many benefits raises an important question. It is not that we do not want to love ourselves. *It is just that we* do not *know how to.*

Despite our understanding of the importance of operating from a place of awareness and accepting and respecting ourselves as we are, while practising kindness and compassion towards ourselves, we often find it challenging due to the presence of obstacles that hinder our self-love. Until we understand and work towards removing these hurdles, self-love will always seem like a far-fetched idea.

# *2*
# BARRIERS TO SELF-LOVE

*'Believing in our hearts that we are enough is the key to a more satisfying and balanced life.'*

**—Ellen Sue Stern**

## 2.1
## Misconceptions about Self-Love

The issue at hand is not a complete absence of self-love, but our struggle to effectively nurture ourselves with love. Individuals seek therapy or coaching when they have reached a stage of profound dissatisfaction, have exhausted all possible efforts to fulfil their needs, and have fallen short of their desired outcomes. They are aware of their present challenges, yet they lack clarity on the specific changes that need to occur and the necessary steps to take. Most of the concerns boil down to certain key ideas and behaviours, which when modified or changed, can drastically improve their quality of life.

Let me take you back to Rashmi's story. When she faced the fact that she had been depriving herself of care and attention, something inside her shifted. When I asked her if she wanted to work on herself to change certain deep-rooted thoughts and behaviour patterns, her answer was an emphatic yes.

In a span of three to four months, Rashmi had:

a. Started following a fitness routine, something she had been longing to do for years but would always defer or leave midway.
b. She took her first solo trip and enjoyed it.

c. She went back to her hobby and found ways to monetise it so she could be financially independent.
d. Started asserting herself and asking for what she wanted instead of being a passive member of the family.

Gradually, she shifted from someone who was always thinking about what others would think or say about her and being perfect all the time, to a person who valued her ideas, opinions, and preferences. All of this and much more became possible for her once she was able to identify and overcome the barriers she was facing. Such are the obstacles that we continue to encounter every day.

When it comes to self-love, there are three major barriers:

- Misconceptions about self-love
- Certain habits and behaviours we constantly engage in
- Mental blocks

We will explore these hurdles in this chapter.

**Misconceptions**

A significant portion of the individuals I work with harbour apprehensions about embracing the concept of self-love, fearing that it will transform them into an undesirable version of themselves. This hesitation stems from the longstanding perception surrounding self-love, which has traditionally been approached in the following manner:

**Misconception 1: Loving Yourself Means Being Selfish and Self-Centred**

**Reality:** We are always taught to put others first to be accepted and treated well by the members of our community, and this is okay because we all want to be loved and accepted by the people around us. However, it often comes at the cost of our own needs—as if we and others cannot coexist on the same plane! People who do things for others without caring for themselves are glorified as if they are doing something great. Yes, serving others is noble but only when it is a choice. If it is carried out of compulsion, there is nothing great about it. Thus, loving yourself means nurturing yourself to be better equipped to care for those around you.

Have you ever noticed firefighters wearing safety gear before entering a burning building? They ensure their safety first to be able to save others. After all, what's the point of jumping to save someone only to die in the process, especially when it is avoidable?

**Misconception 2: Loving Yourself Is Vain**

**Reality:** Loving yourself is not about calling attention to yourself. It is also not about walking around with a placard that reads 'Look at me', 'Talk to me', 'Give me importance!' It is about prioritising self-care by asking yourself, 'What do I need?' and 'How can I better support myself?'

### Misconception 3: If You Ask for What You Want, People May Not Love You and Neglect You

**Reality:** This is a major misconception that keeps people stuck in habitual patterns of disregarding themselves. The fact is that in genuine relationships there is no give or take. People find a way to balance each other's needs and expectations. They will love you when you are at your best and worst. Those who love you will do it regardless of what you do. Genuine and healthy relationships are not transactions; they are built on awareness, acceptance, understanding, and willingness to support each others' needs. If you ask for what you want and someone decides to leave you, that relationship is not worth your time and effort anyway.

### Misconception 4: Loving Yourself Means Not Caring about Others

**Reality:** Wrong! When you learn to love yourself, you can better invest in your relationships. You do the same for others as you become loving and kind towards yourself. This is how self-love enhances your relationships with others. Just like a vehicle cannot run without petrol or diesel, you, too, cannot go on for long without taking care of your own needs.

### Misconception 5: Self-Love Is for Those Who Are into Spirituality

**Reality:** Self-love is open and for all, as each individual needs to nurture themselves. This is a necessary skill and mindset that each one of us needs to cultivate a better life.

### Misconception 6: Self-Love Is about Yoga, Bubble Baths, and Salon Visits

**Reality**: Well, it can be! If these things make you feel better, then why not? Go ahead and pamper yourself with a spa session. Self-care is an extremely important aspect of loving yourself, as you need to recharge now and then. However, it goes beyond physical self-care and includes mental and emotional care as well.

### Misconception 7: Self-Love Will Make You Complacent

**Reality:** On the contrary, love has the power to inspire growth. When you learn to regard yourself, you learn to motivate and encourage yourself as well. You become your own coach and cheerleader.

### Misconception 8: You Cannot Love Another if You Do Not Love Yourself

**Reality:** This is not entirely true. You can and *do* love others. In some cases, you even end up doing more for them. The only problem that arises is that it is not sustainable. Your lack of regard for yourself limits your ability to be fully present for them, increasing your dependence on them.

### Misconception 9: You Must Prove Your Worth or Achieve Something to Love Yourself

**Reality:** We keep laying conditions on love and make it more and more difficult for ourselves. The world of our inner voice often tells us, directly or indirectly, that we are worthy of love only when we have something to show for it, such as a perfect body, grades, job, salary, relationships, awards, etc.

Love is not supposed to be conditional and the same goes for self-love.

If all these ideas are misconceptions, then what does self-love look like? Loving yourself means:

- Putting yourself first wherever needed
- Accepting yourself with all your strengths and areas of improvement
- Not being bothered by what people say or think about you—you choose the people who matter to you and respect and honour their opinions to the best of your ability
- Letting go of your mistakes and learning from them
- Focusing on your thoughts, feelings, and actions
- Taking time out for self-care without feeling guilty

Our process of self-love is hindered by such misconceptions, and it is this fight against them that makes us free from the worldly clutches.

## 2.2

## Unblocking Self-Love: Overcoming Limiting Habits and Behaviours

Once, I posted a story on my social media handle inviting people to share their struggles with self-love. The response was overwhelming and the majority of them listed one or more of the following behaviours they were struggling with and wanted to know why they behaved in such a manner and what was stopping them from changing. The important thing to note is that we all occasionally engage in them to a certain extent. These behaviours become problematic when we are not mindful of when, how, and in what capacity we should engage in them so that they do not interfere with the overall quality of our lives. As you read through these habits, I would appreciate it if you could note down any habits or behaviours that seem relatable to you.

### Constant Self-Criticism

The word 'criticism' means evaluating, assessing, forming a judgement, or expressing disappointment or disapproval towards something or someone. Self-criticism means constantly evaluating, assessing, and judging yourself negatively. In essence, you never approve of yourself; you are constantly finding faults in yourself and your actions.

Certain behaviours are associated with the act of self-criticism:

a. Blaming yourself for every negative situation. If something goes wrong around you, it is always because of you. If someone is having a bad day, it is because of you. If you have not been able to do something, then you are worthless. If something does not go as planned, it becomes your fault.
b. You label your entire personality instead of just looking at the behaviour or situation that needs to be changed. For instance, if you are working on a project and you make a mistake, you will immediately label yourself as stupid, dumb, or incapable instead of thinking, *I made a mistake that needs to be corrected.*

A lot of us believe that self-criticism works as a motivator. However, we often fail to consider the difference between destructive and constructive criticism. Constructive criticism looks at what needs to be improved in the task, situation, or behaviour without attaching any labels or personal judgements about an individual's character or personality. The intention behind this is to provide feedback for growth and development whereas destructive criticism does the opposite. It takes away our ability to improve and focus on avenues for change.

We mostly engage in destructive criticism, and it hampers our inner peace and self-confidence. We believe this kind of criticism keeps us grounded so that we do not let our success get to our heads. But it is all temporary. It may give us the kick we need now, but it leaves us drained and exhausted. Constantly finding faults, using self-defeating labels, and blaming ourselves is like feeding a plant toxins instead of manure to nurture it. just like how the plant eventually perishes, over time, we, too, lose self-confidence and our self-esteem goes for a toss.

### Constant Comparison

Like constructive and destructive criticism, constructive and destructive comparisons are also different. Unfortunately, most of us end up engaging in destructive comparison. We always think of who is better than us in some way or the other. We do not do this exercise to learn anything significant from them but to see what is wrong with us. Once we find our shortcomings, we engage in more self-criticism and judgment. This kind of comparison is detrimental to our emotional and mental well-being.

Comparing ourselves to anyone will always seem unfair because there are no prescriptions for living a perfect human life. Everyone is on their journey, dealing with different circumstances that we know nothing about. When we compare ourselves to others, we rarely consider these differences. We often only consider what is visible on the surface. However, if we do find ourselves comparing, we need to be mindful of the type of comparison we engage in. Destructive comparisons can crush our self-esteem and confidence, leaving us feeling inadequate. On the other hand, constructive comparison is approached mindfully and purposefully.

Let me give you an example. As I mentioned earlier, I struggle with my weight a lot. It took me a long time to truly accept, respect, and love my body the way it is. When

I was not operating from this space of love, I would always look at women who were slim and fit and would end up believing that I could never be like them. It left me deeply disheartened, demotivated, and hopeless. Today, I still look at women who are slim and fit, but now my thought process is that of openness and curiosity. I wonder what is working for them and if there are some things I could try as well. I have also picked up several good habits that have supported my physical health and well-being. Most importantly, I stopped chasing body types, and now I operate from a perspective of healthy and unhealthy.

Constructive comparison enables you to look at others from the lens of curiosity. It empowers you to get inspired and gain information on how to become better in different areas of your life. It helps you understand what would not work for you because of your uniqueness. So, to love yourself more, you need to clean up your lens and develop a perspective that supports your growth.

**Downplaying Your Achievements**

Self-appreciation is one of the main components of self-love and instead of building that up, we do the opposite. So many of us struggle to appreciate or validate our efforts. We keep waiting for someone to show up and pat our backs for our achievements. As a result, we downplay our efforts and achievements because we are afraid of appearing boastful. At other times, we genuinely fail to consider our efforts and victories as significant because we are too busy telling ourselves that whatever we do only matters if someone else validates it. When we do not give due credit to our effort, hard work, and achievements, neither does the world.

For instance, I published my first book in 2017 and apart from a few posts on social media, I did not speak much about it. I did not do much to promote my book. Publishing a book under my name was a dream come true, however, when I finally managed to turn my dream into reality, I did nothing to celebrate it. After the novelty wore off, my dream became 'just another book'. At any event, I prayed for people to not recognise me or bring up my book as I felt uncomfortable talking about my achievements. Slowly, everyone stopped talking about it and my book faded into oblivion. Had I shown some more conviction in my work, things would have been different.

Thus, loving yourself means being able to enjoy your creations and value them, even if they are small because no one else can do what you can.

**Focusing Only on the Negatives**

'Oh, my life sucks!' 'Nothing good ever happens to me!' 'I am a magnet for disaster!' 'There's nothing good about me!'

Are we all not guilty of using these sentences sometimes? Undesirable things happen all around us. Furthermore, we all have our limitations and faults. However, it is important to not focus solely on our shortcomings and ignore the good things in life. According to the principles of neuro-linguistic programming (NLP), our mind is good at three things:

1. **Deletion:** It is the omission of certain parts of our experience. Supposedly, you walk into a party looking your best and you expect people to compliment you. However, you receive only two compliments the entire night. You may have missed out on receiving

compliments because you dismissed the two that you did receive.

2. **Distortion:** It is common for us to modify incoming information to align it with our perceptions, attitudes, beliefs, and expectations. Consequently, when you achieve success in something, you might find yourself attributing it to luck, driven by the belief that there is no inherent goodness within you or that it was merely a rare occurrence, as positive outcomes scarcely come your way.
3. **Generalisation:** We end up making statements or drawing conclusions for every situation based on one experience. Supposedly, if one presentation or event did not go well and you made some mistakes, you are then likely to think that all other similar events will also be disasters. Thus, it is important to be aware of what we learn from our experiences with ourselves, others, and situations. When we focus more on the negative events, incidents, or tendencies within ourselves and others, rather than appreciating and acknowledging the good things that are happening around us, we are only filling ourselves with toxicity. By doing this, rather than nurturing yourself, you are depleting your ability to provide nurturance.

Gradually, this tendency leads to low self-esteem and crippling self-doubt. This constant focus on flaws and mistakes while ignoring or overlooking your strengths and qualities leads to a skewed self-image and a sense of inadequacy.

When people walk into sessions with a strong focus on their negative aspects and I ask them to tell me something they believe is good about them, they often respond with 'I don't know' or 'I don't think there's anything good about me'. Whereas, when I ask them to take some time and list down things that could be their strengths or something people around them have complimented them on, they always come up with at least 10 things! They were so busy focusing on what they could not do that they simply did not look at the other side.

Recognising your shortcomings and being willing to change them is different from dwelling on them. Most of us spend time on the latter. We are neither accepting nor compassionate and feel bad about ourselves and our situation because the focus is rarely on the good.

**Labelling**

Labelling and categorising events, people, and objects is an easy and essential way to make sense of the world. It enables us to organise the world into specific categories that have particular attributes for us to relate to them. It helps reduce chaos and confusion. When we label someone as weird, immature, crazy, adventurous, punctual, organised, or lazy, it provides us with a framework for how to deal with them. We also label ourselves the same way.

However, if we are not conscious of these labels, we can cause ourselves a lot of trouble. Imagine if you are trying to wake up early every day to set a new routine and end up struggling to do so, and after repeated attempts, you end up calling yourself lazy and useless—which also directly ties into your critical and negative self-talk. If you constantly label yourself negatively, you'll end up feeling low, disappointed, and demotivated. Eventually, you will stop trying, deeming yourself to be a failure.

If we are not careful of how we talk to ourselves or the type of labels we use, we will continue to perpetuate a cycle of self-defeating behaviours that keep us from loving ourselves. For instance, you may not wake up early in the morning and that's completely fine. For all you know, you may just not be a morning person, your body may need more rest, or you may have better energy levels in the second half of the day.

Moving past self-judgement will let you figure out an alternate course of action for your struggles.

**Rehashing the Past or Fretting over the Future**

Are you ever afraid that you might lose out on time or won't have enough of it? Do you wonder if certain things had not happened, your life would be different? We all often think about our past in different ways and end up worrying about the future, which is normal. But problems begin to surface when:

a. We constantly think about past events and keep replaying our old hurts, setbacks, or unpleasant memories. When we dwell on those narratives, our tendency to look at everything from a negative lens also increases. We keep complaining about something or the other, which further aggravates our sense of self-doubt and self-criticism. Those past events serve as reference points that shape their actions and decisions throughout their lives. Even though you cannot change the past, you do not have to become its prisoner either. To truly love yourself and move forward in life, you first need to free yourself from the grip of your past.

b. We are perpetually worried about the future. This often leads to overthinking and being preoccupied with negative scenarios. This, once again, leads to persistent self-doubt.

Occasionally visiting these time zones is okay, however, these are not the right places to stay in. In one time zone, things have already happened, and in the other, they are yet to happen. What remains is now. If you want to cultivate self-love, you must do it now, in the present, because that's all that you have. You can only learn from those past stories and work now to create the future you desire.

**Not Setting Boundaries**

'Half of the troubles of this life can be traced to saying yes too quickly and not saying no soon enough.' I remember this quote by Josh Billings when I struggled to set boundaries by saying 'no' to things I did not want to do. To please people around us, keep them happy, and be in their good books, we often compromise ourselves. We put ourselves in unpleasant situations, only to be filled with regret later. We take on more than we can handle, fail to voice our concerns, and eventually open ourselves to a lot of disrespect, bad behaviour, and being taken for granted.

Loving yourself means being able to set boundaries against such toxic environments without feeling guilty or anxious about others' perceptions.

**Giving up Your Needs**

You cannot love yourself if you do not honour your needs, wants, and desires because doing so is a reminder that you understand, accept, respect, and care for yourself. Honouring your needs is an extremely significant aspect of self-care. We all have different needs—physical, emotional, social, psychological, and spiritual— that are important, which we must fulfil. Unfortunately, we do not pay much attention to them. We often do not even take care of our basic physical needs like food, water, and rest because we are busy putting somebody else's needs above our own.

This reminds me of an incident that occurred a few years ago. Once, I visited a relative's house with my family for dinner and ended up chit-chatting with the host's daughter-in-law. I noticed that while she was busy serving food and taking care of the guests, she was not eating or drinking anything herself. I offered to get her something, but she vehemently refused. I was taken aback by her reaction and couldn't help myself but ask her if everything was okay. She told me that she had been recently married and wanted to make a good impression on everyone. She was worried about what people would think about her. She was not eating or drinking to come across as the quintessential good daughter-in-law. Exhaustion and hunger were written all over her face, but she was adamant about not eating or resting.

Almost a year later, she approached me for therapy sessions as by then she had completely lost track of her life. She had put on weight, developed sleeping issues, had anxiety, and was brimming with self-doubt. She had compromised her physical, emotional, and psychological needs altogether. With time, she had given up being who she was as she desperately tried to fit into a mould that was not meant for her. She took a stand for herself and was afraid of upsetting her in-laws with her views and opinions, however suffocated she felt.

The truth is, we are all guilty of doing this at one point or the other. We believe giving up our needs to please people automatically makes us eligible to be regarded as important and worthy. We think this will make everyone around us take care of us because we are doing so much for them. Only if the equations in life were so simple!

For others to take care of our needs, it requires an awareness of:

- Our needs
- How those fulfilled needs look and feel for us
- Who can support us in meeting those needs in the best way possible
- Alternate options in case those needs are not met

**Not Taking out Time for Self-Care**

Do you sleep enough and eat well enough? Do you ask for what you want without feeling guilty or embarrassed about it? If you do, you are on the right track. If not, it is time to step back and think.

We all *know* that self-care in any form is important, but how many of us implement it? At some level, we glorify putting aside our needs and doing things for others because that makes us 'appear' good for the role. When we compromise on our self-care more than necessary, it costs us in various ways. I work with many individuals who live on one meal a day or ten cups of coffee because they are 'busy doing the things they are supposed to'.

While they look great at the role they are playing, they perish as individuals. The worst part of this habit is the expectation, 'I am doing so much for everyone so they should understand what I am going through and give me what I need.' This sets the ball rolling for numerous disasters in different directions. No one else is responsible for you or your needs—that is why you are an adult and not a child. Therefore, meeting your needs will always be your responsibility and this extends to the people you choose to keep in your lives as well.

### Not Receiving Compliments

Even though we all want to feel good about ourselves and be loved and appreciated for who we are, criticism, comparison, and negative bias keep us from appreciating ourselves. Whenever we do something good, we are quick to negate our contributions.

Some of us rarely tell ourselves 'I like what I have done' or 'I look good!' and are surprised to see someone else appreciating themselves. Similarly, when someone reaches out to compliment us, we either minimise the importance of our efforts by saying things like 'Oh, but I did not do much' or 'It just happened by chance' or we end up taking a dig at ourselves.

Other times, while we may not say anything to anyone on the surface, we dismiss the compliment in our mind by questioning it, negating its importance, or making fun of ourselves.

Being able to compliment yourself and accepting it from others is not only a part of self-appreciation but an important element of self-love as well. We all like receiving compliments, so why don't we learn to accept them graciously?

### Not Asserting Yourself

Which of the following statements is true for you most of the time?

a. I can take a stand, communicate effectively and express my opinions.
b. I tend to avoid, ignore, and escape important conversations and discussions.
c. I react very strongly in a conflict, disagreement, or argument.

If the first statement feels more aligned with you, you are doing a good job. However, if you find yourself leaning towards the second and third statements, you should reassess yourself. A key component of loving yourself is being assertive, i.e., expressing and communicating effectively. Assertive communication includes being responsive rather than reactive. It is to state your boundaries, likes, and dislikes with respect for yourself as well as the other person.

However, when we experience a lack of self-love, we are mostly reactive with our actions, swinging between being passive and aggressive. When we are passive, we let issues slide, give up our needs, and allow ourselves to be taken for granted, making us feel suffocated. We suppress our thoughts and emotions to maintain peace. Eventually, we reach a point where we cannot hold it in and explode. Consequently, we start resenting not only others but ourselves, too.

Similarly, when we are aggressive in our expression and communication, we try to overpower, control, or dominate people. We become rigid and fail to resolve any issues or concerns. Gradually, this strains our relationships because we begin to take away everyone's space.

Being assertive is crucial for healthy interactions and relationships. Being reactive and aggressive may make it difficult for people to ignore or overlook you, but they will never be comfortable around you.

In both cases, we end up damaging the emotional connection essential for our relationships to thrive. Therefore, we need to express ourselves healthily through self-love.

## Hesitant to Ask for Help

So many of us struggle to ask for help; some do not even try. Most of us would jump to help others even if costs us a great deal, but we wouldn't step up for ourselves when we need it the most. While being able to help and support others is wonderful, it does not have to be at the cost of self-sacrifice. This is a sign of a lack of self-love because those who are unable to ask for help, do not want to appear as a burden to others. They want to maintain the façade of having everything in control. They would rather be the go-to person for everyone rather than reach out for support themselves.

This lack of love makes it difficult for you to put yourself first and ask for what you want. If you ever need support, you are likely to end up thinking that you are not good enough because you cannot do things on your own.

On the other hand, when you come from a space of self-love, you are better attuned to your strengths, qualities, and areas of improvement. You recognise when something is too much for you, and to better take care of yourself, you are willing to ask for support. After all, we all need help as nobody can do everything on their own all the time.

## Feeling Guilty

This is perhaps the biggest struggle we face when we do not love ourselves enough. Anything we do for ourselves is overshadowed by a huge sense of guilt, which makes it extremely uncomfortable for us to ask ourselves for our needs. Somewhere we believe that it is not okay for us to be who we are, have needs, or ask for what we want.

Thus, our behaviour of giving up our needs, not taking out time for self-care, and avoiding asking for help persists. Over time, it becomes too much to bear. We need to understand the concept of self-love a bit more deeply to support ourselves and overcome these difficult emotions.

**Not Feeling Body Confident**

Your body is a representation of your personality. If you do not love yourself enough, you wouldn't love your body either. It is difficult to find people who accept, love, and treat their bodies with respect.

Our body does more than just look a certain way. Unfortunately, we are too preoccupied with the looks part of it, and when it does not meet certain standards, we end up comparing, criticising, neglecting, and mistreating our bodies. Most of us disapprove of the way our bodies look, 'I don't like how I look' or 'I hate how I look'. No matter how tall or short you are or which side of the weighing scale you are on, this is an outlook shared by most of us.

All of us are chasing the ideal of a perfect body without realising that it does not exist. Yes, certain elements of our body can be enhanced, changed, or improved, but even that should be exercised out of self-love and in the interest of our highest good, not because we are part of a mindless struggle to be like someone else.

Being able to love yourself includes loving your body just the way it is. It involves creating a space of love and acceptance for this vehicle that keeps you going. However, loving your body should not be seen as an excuse to be complacent about issues. For instance, if you need to make certain lifestyle changes, such as gaining or losing weight, you need to address them out of love and concern for your health rather than letting them fester under the guise of self-love. When we love ourselves, we can recognise the immense value our body carries and treat it with respect, care, and compassion.

### Being Uncomfortable with Your Emotions

Many of us are uncomfortable exploring our emotions. We want to do everything in our power to make them go away, and we find ways to ignore and dismiss them. While it is true that a lot of us lack the skills for emotional management, we do not exactly know what to do when we experience uncomfortable emotions such as sadness and emptiness. Furthermore, we feel embarrassed while experiencing such emotions. We exhaust ourselves by trying to build our lives feeling good, happy, and in control always. We fail to recognise that genuine self-love involves embracing both light and darkness within. It is about loving yourself even in your weak, vulnerable moments and treating yourself with compassion instead of labelling yourself as weak, incapable, or a loser.

Love does not need you to look or be a certain way. You simply need to love yourself regardless of love's appearance.

### Chasing Perfection

What is perfection anyway?

We are always chasing this ideal without realising that it does not exist. Everything is flawed. There are cracks in everything we see. As humans, we are a bundle of mistakes and mishaps. Yet, we fall prey to the idea that we can be perfect and do things faultlessly. We keep pushing ourselves up the wall by chasing one goal after the other, trying to get everything right, and making no mistakes to prove that we can be worthy of being loved. We then end up setting unrealistic expectations for ourselves as well as others, and failure to meet any of these throws us into a deep, dark pit of self-doubt, inadequacy, and worthlessness.

In the words of Hugh Prather, 'Perfectionism is a slow death . . . If everything were to turn out just like I would want it to, just like I would plan for it to, then I would never experience anything new; my life would be an endless repetition of stale successes. When I make a mistake, I experience something unexpected . . . when I have listened to my mistakes I have grown.'

A huge part of loving yourself is to drop the need to be perfect and cease chasing the ideal of perfection. Give your best in everything that you do but learn to make room for flaws because that is where growth takes place.

### *Exercise #1: Self-Love Quotient*

Before moving on to the next part, I would like you to spend a few moments and take this test to check your self-love quotient.

Read each statement and choose the answer that fits your description the best. If your response to the statements is yes, then you are on the path to self-love, if your response to most of these statements is no, it is time to love yourself more, and if your response to most of them is sometimes, you are on the path of self-love and need to keep at it.

| STATEMENT | YES | NO | SOMETIMES |
|---|---|---|---|
| I appreciate myself. | | | |
| I can let go of my mistakes. | | | |
| I prioritise my health and well-being by taking out time for self-care. | | | |
| I can ask for help when I need it. | | | |
| I regularly take out time for self-reflection. | | | |
| I am fine with my areas of imperfections and shortcomings. | | | |
| I love and respect my body. I treat it well by taking care of it. | | | |

| STATEMENT | YES | NO | SOMETIMES |
|---|---|---|---|
| I am aware of my strengths and qualities and can easily harness them. | | | |
| I don't give up my needs, wants, and dreams for others. I can balance both. | | | |
| I can say no and establish boundaries when needed. | | | |
| I am comfortable with my emotions. | | | |
| I am comfortable with receiving compliments. | | | |

## 2.3
## Hidden Blocks to Self-Love

Human behaviour is complex, dynamic, and multi-layered. Just when you think you know all about yourself, there's a new layer waiting to be uncovered. All the aforementioned habits and behaviours are only the tip of the iceberg. They are the outer manifestation of something else that's going on within. These behaviours are our attempts at getting some of our core fundamental needs met as human beings.

We want to be seen, heard, and validated for who we are. We want to know that our existence matters. We matter.

Thus, we set out on a quest to get someone to fill this void, which constantly nags us, 'Do I matter?' 'Am I important?' 'Am I loved and understood for who I am?' To fill this void, we chase after people and goals, hoping to feel valued. Our mental vessel is empty, and we hope for someone else to fill it up.

Consequently, we engage in behaviours that push us to chase external love to fill this void, which leads to destructive behaviours, harming us and filling us with anger, frustration, and resentment. This is not love, as true love brings peace, harmony, satisfaction, and empowerment. It should uplift, not destroy. In each of these behaviours, we are minimising or letting go of essential components of our existence, hoping and wishing that someone will see this compromise and give us what we need or deserve. A large part of learning to love yourself requires uncovering these hidden blocks within so that you can let them go and fill yourself with the kind of love that you want and need.

We must learn to love ourselves and others in ways that truly feel like love and do not cause us to lose ourselves in the process.

# 3
# UNCOVERING THE HIDDEN BLOCKS OF SELF-LOVE

*'Be the love you never received.'*

**—Rune Lazuli**

# 3.1
# Twisted Ways of the Mind

I vividly remember one of the therapy sessions with my therapist, where she drew an unusual diagram about the mind and explained to me where my anxiety stemmed from and why. That diagram did not make perfect sense to me then. I sat there, puzzled as to how this could be true. How was it that my mind was creating this anxiety, and if I changed the way I thought about certain things, it would impact my anxiety levels as well? That seemed a bit bizarre. I was perfectly fine and had everything under control, while someone was telling me that I had acute anxiety. I couldn't absorb it.

Years later, I am the one who is drawing that weird-looking diagram for my clients, helping them understand where their thoughts and behaviour patterns originate from. Life comes full circle.

My journey into my mind began shortly after I started facing issues during my postgraduation. Some things in my life were under my control up until I graduated. I had taken up a subject—Psychology—I was finally doing well in. I was struggling a bit but doing decently well. I had my moments when I would be gripped by this intense anxiety before any submission or exam. I was a nervous wreck when it came to studies and tended to drive myself—and sometimes others—up the wall. Even though I had found some confidence during the last two years of school, I was back to feeling small in college.

Everyone was better, smarter, more confident, and knowledgeable, while I felt like a lost puppy. Additionally, I sustained a major head injury that led to other issues in my upper back, which obstructed my daily functioning. That became another cause for anxiety. Somehow, I managed to go through those three difficult years of graduation, and soon, it was time to take the next logical step, i.e., enrolling in a postgraduation programme. This was where the problem started.

By the time I graduated, I was doing poorly both mentally and physically for two reasons. First, while I was good at Psychology, I was more inclined towards media studies and other creative pursuits. I wanted to dance, write, and sing. I applied to all the top colleges and universities for the same and got admission to one of them. But I had to let it go because of my urgent health issues. Second, my injury had impacted my back tremendously, and by the end of my graduation, I was in such bad shape that I had trouble performing everyday tasks. I was diagnosed with Fibromyalgia, which has no cure or treatment and can only be managed.

My medical condition had left me incapacitated in so many aspects that envisioning a life had become challenging. I had to give up certain ambitions because I knew that I wouldn't be able to manage them with my present physical and mental condition. I was heartbroken. It felt as if my life had ended even before it started. Dealing with all of this, along with several other things that were happening simultaneously, took a huge toll on me. It was then that I decided to take a year-long sabbatical.

I wanted to take time off, reconsider my decisions, and find treatment options for my condition. During the break, all my peers had settled into their respective master's courses. Some had moved out of India to study and were having a blast. While I was here, sitting in this mess, feeling lost, miserable, and hopeless about my life. To top it all, I had enrolled in a short-term media course, which did not work out well either. After more than half of the year had passed, I finally decided to go abroad, following in the footsteps of some of my batchmates, to pursue a master's degree in psychology. I applied to a couple of universities in the United Kingdom and got through all of them. All I had to do was choose from the long list.

Amongst all the universities, one was renowned and prestigious, based in London. Going there was a no-brainer. But my heart was not in it. My gut kept telling me to choose another one. However, since this was the most logical, socially appropriate choice to make, I chose to go there.

I remember, there were multiple signs, indicating that this was not the right choice for me. Yet, I ignored all of them and went to study there. What should have been the start of an upward climb, turned into a massive downward spiral. My breakdowns started on the first day I reached my accommodation in London. I felt like I was suddenly hit by a giant vacuum that had come out of nowhere. I hated every minute of it. I neither liked the course nor my accommodation. My anxiety levels were through the roof, making it impossible for me to socialise with my classmates.

I was constantly overwhelmed and felt insignificant, insecure, and useless in front of everyone. The simplest of things seemed extremely complicated. I tried hard to cope by involving myself in projects and assignments, but everything increased my anxiety. I had then become an insomniac as well. Eventually, I reached a point where I would begin my day by crying and end it the same way. I just couldn't take it anymore and wanted to quit; however, the fear of disappointing everyone was overwhelming. I thought of myself as the biggest fool in the history of human existence—to think of dropping out of an excellent university and course, and I was sure that everyone thought the same!

I dropped out eventually and returned home only to come back to a sea of disappointed faces. My parents had worked hard to support my educational endeavour only for me to come back as a failure. Finally, I reached out to my therapist for help. I spent the next two years covering up for my failures by throwing myself into another master's degree in India. Even though I was faring well, I was riddled with severe anxiety, sleep, and digestive issues in addition to my pre-existing fibromyalgia. I continued to see my therapist on the side to gain some control over my life. That's when, one fine day, she decided to tell me about the inner workings of my mind and how I had, unknowingly, created certain patterns for myself that were blocking my way of accomplishing anything, preventing me from leading a quality life. As I continued to dig deeper with the help of my therapist and another mentor, I came face to face with subconscious issues that were giving rise to those behaviours and maintaining them.

With time, I have come to understand that getting on this journey of self-love requires an understanding of three crucial aspects:

i. How your mind works
ii. How your experiences have shaped you
iii. Your narrative about yourself

These are important because, believe it or not, as Buddha had said, 'Our life is the creation of our mind'. You cannot control everything that happens to you, only the interpretations and conclusions you draw from it.

## 3.2
## Say Hello to Your Mind

What is the mind? This question has fascinated scientists and researchers for decades. Many of them view the mind and brain as two aspects of the same phenomenon, with the mind emerging from the brain's complex activity of the neurons and synapses. The systematic study of the mind goes back to the Ancient Greeks—Plato and Aristotle—who tried to understand and explain the nature of the human mind.

As the field of Psychology gained prominence around the 19th century, several schools of Psychology emerged with their definition and understanding of the mind. It remains an intriguing topic. However, for our understanding, we will keep it simple and not turn this into a Psychology class.

To begin with, let us first understand that we have a brain, which is a physical organ, observed and studied through techniques like neuroimaging. The mind is a more complex and abstract concept that is difficult to define and measure. While there are various theories of the mind, including the infamous Iceberg Model by Dr Sigmund Freud, I will talk about one that's a bit short and easy to understand. This theory was proposed by Dr John Kappas, a prominent psychologist, hypnotherapist, author, and educator who had made significant contributions to the field of psychotherapy and hypnotherapy.

According to his theory, the human mind is divided into two major parts—the conscious and the subconscious. The conscious mind cares for one's logical thinking, decision-making, and problem-solving. The active and alert part of the mind makes up for 12 per cent of our entire mind. This part is aware of everything that is happening within you. On the other hand, your subconscious mind, which constitutes the remaining 88 per cent of your mind, takes care of everything happening within you, but you unaware of its working. It operates below the level of conscious awareness and is responsible for processing emotions, memories, and other information not directly accessible to the conscious thought.

We also have the primitive mind, which is a part of the subconscious mind, which exists at the time of birth and contains our basic survival responses such as flight, fight, freeze, and inborn reflexes to loud noises or falling. Between the conscious and subconscious, rests the critical filter that is typically formed between the ages of 0–5 years and consists of rules and beliefs required to lead our lives. Thus, what we think we know about ourselves is only 12 per cent and a large chunk of information lies within the subconscious, completely hidden from our awareness.

Even though the basic workings of the mind are the same for everyone, there are individual differences in how each one of us perceives the world. We constantly receive truckloads of information from the world through our senses, but our mind creates its understanding and interpretation around the given information. You must have heard of the 'glass half-full, half-empty' proverbial phrase. This means that we all view the world differently, which, in turn, impacts how we think, feel, and respond to every person or situation we come across. At times, we are aware of what's happening, and, at others, we may be completely clueless. This understanding of our mind is essential because even on a day-to-day basis, there are several thoughts, emotions, and behaviours we engage in that we do not know about.

When we talk about the so-called struggle between the heart and the mind, it is the struggle between the conscious (logic) and the subconscious (emotion). When our logic and emotions are aligned, we feel stable and connected with ourselves. There is a sense of direction and purpose in our actions. However, problems arise when they move in opposite directions.

Through my inner work during and after my master's degree, I understood that a major disconnection between my conscious and subconscious led to the entire master's fiasco. It was quite simple—I made the logical choice of going to a prestigious university while subconsciously, I wanted to go somewhere else. However, my tendency to try and be perfect, do the right thing, make the right choice, and fear of disappointing people made me choose otherwise. I pushed myself to accept this decision even though my heart was not in it, and I made the wrong choice. Eventually, I created the circumstance I always wanted to avoid—trying not to disappoint anyone. Then I spent the rest of my years covering up my failures by adopting more self-destructive patterns. Eventually, I found it hard to switch off.

I came back to India and enrolled in a master's degree. In a bid to compensate for the London debacle, I pushed myself to perform well, which extracted a huge cost, and I did not realise this until later. I kept doing similar things in other areas of my life as well. It was only when I became aware of my actions that I turned things around. Yet, there was a lot to be uncovered.

## 3.3
## Digging Deeper

Life would be much easier if we only had to learn a couple of theories, right? Now that you know how your mind works, you can easily control it and steer it in whichever direction you want to. Right? Well, it is certainly true in theory, however, it's not something that you can do in just one or even a few days! Most of us struggle within ourselves because we are unaware of what is happening in our minds. Knowing about the different parts of your mind and working with them are not necessarily mutually exclusive. Even though I understood a lot about the inner workings of my mind, my patterns did not change overnight.

I became more aware of how my patterns were spilling into other areas, such as relationships, health, body image, and career. It was driving me crazy! By the time I finished postgraduation, I was still a mess. I had a gold medal that I couldn't care less about, and my parents were proud of me, but it mattered little. My body and spirit were shattered as I pushed myself beyond my capacity, and there were some things I couldn't control. I had to finish my education if I wanted a good career, which had always been important for me. But the way I worked for it was problematic. Furthermore, I did not get any relevant treatment and my symptoms kept flaring up. By the end of this phase, my therapist had moved out of the country, making me feel lost and dejected.

Life continued some or the other way for another two years without any hope. I was physically incapacitated because my health issues had progressed. I was in no condition to do anything, and I no longer had a purpose in life. The only thing that I could do well was watch television and sleep. Since I could not do much, I found myself turning towards spirituality and alternate modalities like tarot and numerology. That's how I found my mentor. By the time I reached out to him, I had given up on everything. There was no respite for my symptoms, no one was able to understand what was going on, and my mental health needed a lot of help. My issues with my parents had become quite apparent as we couldn't sit in the same room for five minutes without arguing. I was facing issues with every person in my life. My mentor introduced me to the world of healing. I was only focusing on the symptoms, and it took me time to understand that those symptoms were not the problem; they were only the manifestation of the problem.

Imagine waking up with a stomach ache. What will you do? You will probably pop a painkiller or two and go about your day. However, if the pain persists, you will start to worry and continue to come up with fixes for the same. Now, if you experience more symptoms as the day progresses, like nausea and diarrhoea, you will reach out to a doctor. Upon proper investigation, the doctor will probably tell you that you have a stomach infection that needs to be treated and give you appropriate medication. You take those antibiotics and feel better in a few days as the infection and symptoms subside. The mind works the same. Your subconscious creates discomfort in the form of anxiety, worry, mood, and energy changes. It also leads to severe body aches, pains, muscle tightness, digestive issues and much more to draw attention to something that lies underneath.

At times, discomfort manifests as feelings of dissatisfaction being troubled by the same pattern of behaviour you have engaged in for years, but suddenly, something about them begins to feel off. Something along similar lines happened with one of my clients.

Sara: 'I have been sick for the last three weeks. I had a throat infection, then severe hair fall, and then my gut went for a toss! And you know, I have just started my new job and I hate to be looked upon as one of those lazy, incompetent people who keep taking days off from work. Oh, and my anxiety has been so bad as well. I cannot sleep, I am working all night, and I have this constant chatter in my head that keeps telling me: "Sara you better get your act together and work! Look at you! You look so pathetic! Who would ever want to be with you?" Ugh . . . I am so tired of all this. I need to take a break, but I cannot seem to do that.'

Me: 'And what's stopping you from taking a break?'

Sara (after a careful pause): Well, nothing. I mean, I can take a break if I want to.

Me: 'But what about your new job and all the commitments?'

Sara: 'Oh, the people at my new job are quite understanding and they cut me slack since I fell sick immediately after joining. My work offers me the flexibility to work from anywhere.'

Me: 'Okay, so if they are supportive and can understand your situation, then what's coming in the way of taking a break?'

Sara: 'Umm, I think it is . . . me.'

Me: 'Hmm.'

Sara: 'I know we have talked about this, but I don't think I paid much attention to it earlier. But I am realising now that I am unable to stop pushing myself, and my self-talk is terrible. I remember in one of our sessions you had told me something about the mind-body connection and that if we are stressed or anxious it has physical manifestations as well. I think I can see that now. When my anxiety levels go up, my hair fall increases. As I am working round the clock, I don't let myself sleep on time, which is now leading to more anxiety and other digestive issues. I am consulting an Ayurveda practitioner for my hair loss and digestion-related issues, and he agreed with you.'

Me: 'So, what do you think your body is trying to tell you through all these issues?'

Sara (laughs): 'Oh, well, it's telling me to slow down and take proper care of myself. At this rate, I will burn out in the next 2–3 years. I need to find my off button.' But [after a brief pause], I am also afraid.'

Me: 'What are you afraid of?'

Sara: 'Afraid that if I do slow down, I would neither be myself nor be able to do all the things that matter to me or make me, me, you know?'

Me: 'And what makes you, you?'

Sara: 'This! Overworking, being on top of my game all the time, knowing all the answers to everything, and being successful at what I do.'

Me: 'And where did you get this idea that to be successful you need to overwork yourself and not take a break at all?'

Sara: 'Well, I have grown up listening to how you always

need to work hard, how you shouldn't rest until you finish everything, and how you shouldn't compliment yourself because then it will go to your head. If you want to be perceived as good, you have got to work hard for it!'

By then she had broken down. However, she continued to talk even as she was crying and went on to say, 'I wish I could just find a way to slow down and rest. I want to be able to tell myself that I am good even if I am not doing anything. I have this strong idea that if I stop working, I wouldn't be of any value anymore and I feel the same in my relationships—I must look good, dress well, and be perfect—otherwise, no one will want to be with me. And I am tired of feeling this way, but I don't know how to get out of this.'

There it was, hidden beneath all her symptoms, the driving force that showed up in the form of 'I won't be successful, valued, and loved if I don't have something to show for it,' constantly keeping her on high alert.

Our mind is like an iceberg. What is visible to us is only a fraction of what lies underneath, and it takes a lot of self-reflection, introspection, curiosity, and the ability to sit with discomfort and dig all of that out. Usually, the driving force behind all our actions is our beliefs about ourselves, others, and everything in the world. Belief is the feeling of being certain that something exists or is true.

Look at all this debate about whether God exists or not. Some say God exists and some do not. What is that? A difference in what people consider to be the truth. Beliefs are our versions of the truth, and I say that because there is no absolute truth. You and I see the world differently and can have different ideas about the same thing. When it comes to loving yourself, whether you do or do not, depends on the belief you hold about yourself. What do these beliefs look like?

If you take a paper and pen and complete the sentence: 'I am . . .', you will realise that what you are putting down are your beliefs. When we say things like 'I am smart, confident, intelligent, good-looking, loved, cared for' or 'I am an ugly, incapable, stupid, dumb, loser, no one loves me, I am good for nothing,' these are all beliefs. In essence, they are your reality.

Likewise, you have beliefs about every individual, relationship, and object that is connected with you. If you believe life is hard, you need to work hard to be successful, self-love is selfish, and money does not grow on trees, that is what you will manifest in your behaviour. Some beliefs will be healthy and functional, which will assist you in nourishing yourself, and there will also be several self-limiting beliefs that will act as roadblocks to loving yourself, keeping you in the loop of self-destructive habits and behaviours.

If we go back to Sara's story, we see how her belief that 'I will be valued if I worked hard enough' was preventing her from slowing down, engaging in constructive self-talk, and taking better care of herself. While it gave her success, accolades, and appreciation, it was taking away her mental peace, emotional balance, and overall health. It was then upon her to choose whether she wanted to continue operating from this belief or change it.

Thus, before we look at changing a belief, we first need to understand how these self-limiting beliefs form so that we can unlearn certain things before learning new ones.

### *Exercise #2: Identify Your Beliefs*

Take some time out to reflect on the ideas or beliefs that you possess about the following aspects of your life. As you read each category, complete the statements in at least five different ways. Write what comes to your mind in a flow.

I think/believe:

1. Life is

______________________________________________

______________________________________________

______________________________________________

______________________________________________

______________________________________________

2. Relationships are

______________________________________________

______________________________________________

______________________________________________

______________________________________________

______________________________________________

3. Money is

______________________________________________

______________________________________________

______________________________________________

______________________________________________

______________________________________________

4. Parents are

5. I am

## 3.4

## Understanding the Origin of Beliefs

A belief is nothing more than a thought you have repeatedly heard or recited yourself. Beliefs are extremely important because they act as the mental shortcuts required to make sense of the enormous amounts of information that are coming your way. Beliefs categorise certain things for ease and convenience. Our mind then uses those beliefs as a template for all the other pieces of information. Our beliefs help us to make sense of the world. They enable us to determine the kind of actions we should or shouldn't engage in. For instance, I do not drive. I am terrified of driving because, while learning, I got into a series of mishaps that tanked my already low confidence. Every time I made a mistake, my inner voice would pop up and tell me, 'See, you are not good at this! You are a bad driver. You are incompetent!' Back then, I was unaware of my internal voice. Thus, I never realised the impact this negative self-talk had on me. It also got reinforced when someone around me mocked or passed a snide comment like 'She needs to learn. She has a long way to go.' It always reminded me

of those report cards in school that read: 'She has potential. She needs to work hard.' Gradually, I lost interest in driving because of my beliefs.

Furthermore, when I tried to drive a few times, they were near disasters. My anxiety got the better of me every time, and I still haven't found the courage to restart. However, an interesting part about beliefs is that not all beliefs need to be changed or worked upon. Sometimes, a belief may be self-limiting, but it may not have a significant impact on your life. For example, my belief about my ability as a driver does not impact my day-to-day functioning. I can work with other means of transportation and my life is not influenced by it to a large extent.

In effect, we have several functional and self-limiting beliefs that coexist and operate at various levels. If they are not creating chaos, we can let them be. However, if an idea or belief starts to come in the way of self-love and impacts the quality of our lives, we need to pay attention to it.

Let us go back to Sara's story for a bit. During our later conversation, I inquired about the source of her belief that she had to work hard to be appreciated. I also asked her about her tendency to focus more on her shortcomings rather than her accomplishments. She told me that growing up that was what she had constantly heard from her parents. They mentored her to do more, do better, work harder, and not rest. They warned her that if she had to make a place for herself in the world, she needed to be her best. Whenever she made a mistake or did not do well, things were particularly difficult for her. On the other hand, when she did well, she was not complimented or appreciated enough. There were not any celebrations or treats because doing well was simply expected of her. She grew up with a void within—a constant thought that she would never be at par, never be enough no matter what she does. Everything was about proving herself to the world, even though she believed otherwise. Now that this had impacted her negatively, it was time to change.

Before moving towards changing a belief, it is important to acknowledge, accept, and understand its roots because then we are no longer looking at just a symptomatic approach. Instead, we are looking at healing and learning

to love ourselves requires us to look at the beliefs that are blocking our way like weeds. We must then uproot them and plant new seeds of self-love that lead to healthy behaviours and practices towards the self.

## 3.5

## UNRAVELLING THE SOURCES AND INFLUENCES THAT SHAPE BELIEFS

Have you ever noticed how curious babies are about everything in the world including themselves? When babies are born, they have no idea of who is around them or what is happening in the world. They have no sense of right, wrong, good, or bad. They do not even know about their body parts. They approach everything with pure joy, excitement, and curiosity. Most importantly, they love their bodies. Babies have no pragmatic concepts about anything, and they live by their basic survival needs and programmed reflexes. So, when a baby is hungry, thirsty, or in some discomfort, it cries or becomes irritable to let the adult know that it needs to be attended to. Just like a baby has basic physical needs, it also has basic emotional needs such as the need to be seen, heard, validated, loved, and taken care of. These needs are a part of our physiology as human beings.

Besides that, a baby's mind is like a blank slate, unaware as to how to navigate this big, scary adult world. Thus, it is dependent physically, emotionally, and intellectually on the adults around to make sense of the world. Its self-concept relies heavily on the information and feedback that it receives from the primary caregivers and other adults. As a young, helpless, dependent being, a large part of a child's development is centred around figuring out its identity in the world. Children want to know if their presence or absence matters—they want to be heard and feel understood; loved and accepted for who they are.

Through the course of a child's development, they constantly receive different types of inputs from the environment about every aspect of their being—face, body, attitude, behaviour, conduct, etc. Some inputs are positive, some are not. If the negative inputs tend to be more intense or frequent, they end up creating certain self-limiting beliefs, which, in turn, have the power to override the positive ones. What also aids this entire process is the fact that our mind naturally gravitates towards the negative. This has been a part of our physiology ever since primitive times. The only difference now is that the human mind has become more evolved and sophisticated and the kind of threats that we face today are different from those of earlier times. Now we must grapple with threats such as not being loved, not being treated as important, being abandoned, not being financially independent or secure, not having met certain milestones in life, and much more. Earlier, we had wild animals like lions and bears to be afraid of, now we only see them in books or on the Discovery Channel. Therefore, if negative inputs overshadow positive ones, they create self-limiting beliefs that exert a more powerful influence on our identity.

If you grew up listening to things like 'You are not as smart or intelligent as your sibling or your peers,' 'You need to work harder,' 'You are not good enough,' 'You wouldn't be able to become successful in life,' 'No one would want to be with a child like you if you keep behaving this way,' either directly or indirectly, they would make up for a large part of your belief system. For instance, I grew up listening to statements like, 'She needs to work hard' or 'Look at other children, they are doing so well. You should also be like them. Results matter the most.' These made me adopt a workhorse mentality. It also led me to believe that, in the end, those very efforts do not matter, only the result does. Since I was never achieving any 'good results' and was not valuing my efforts, my mind created the belief that I was never and will never be good enough. This mindset also led me to start and abandon several endeavours because I could never truly enjoy the process; I was always worried about the result.

Thus, it is said that the formative years of a child's development are extremely important. As adults, we need to be careful about the inputs we provide to a child. If a child grows up in an environment filled with emotional or physical neglect, criticism, comparison, abandonment, and abuse, these experiences can turn out to be extremely painful and traumatic for a helpless, dependent being to process. To cope with everything occurring in the child's environment, their mind starts to look for ways to meet their needs.

Now, the interesting part about being a human is that right from childhood, our world is driven largely by two things:

i. Our beliefs are the conclusions that we draw about everything so that we can find ways to cope.
ii. Our needs are necessary for survival at all levels.

It is this constant interaction between our beliefs and needs that provides meaning to life. Your belief is the fuel that lets you reach your destination, which is your need(s) at a given time. Behaviours such as people-pleasing, seeking validation, not being able to set boundaries, criticism, comparison, swinging between passive and aggressive behaviour, not taking time out for self-care, and thinking that self-love is selfish are coping mechanisms that our mind uses to enable us to meet our emotional, psychological, and physical needs.

Psychiatrist Dr Conrad Baars and Dr Anna Terruwe, in their book *Healing the Unaffirmed*, based on their research on the impact of emotional deprivation on human development, write, 'A human being's emotional life evolves only gradually from infancy until adulthood. Progressing from one stage to the next can be so only if the lower stage has reached its full development through adequate gratification of its natural needs. This gratification is necessary for entering into the next stage of emotional development. No phase of growth can be skipped, for only the satisfactory completion and perfection of one phase prepares the child for the next one.'

They further explain that if a child's emotional needs are not met due to external factors, their emotions will continuously seek out the necessary gratification they need. Without this, the child's emotional development will be hindered, and they will struggle to progress to a higher level of emotional maturity. In essence, we cannot learn to love ourselves on our own while growing up. We need someone else to love us first to build our sense of identity and love around it. This presence or absence of love from the world around us becomes our definition of self-love.

If the love we receive is broken, damaged, or filled with cracks then it is difficult for us to grow around it fully and healthily. We carry that damaged version of love within us, which we pass on to others as well. As Louise Hay wrote in her book *You Can Heal Your Life*, 'We are all victims of victims, and they could not possibly have taught us anything they did not know. If your mother did not know how to love herself, or your father did not know how to love himself, then it would be impossible for them to teach you to love yourself.

They were doing the best they could with what they had been taught as children . . . Those people who "did all that stuff to you" were just as frightened as you are.'

Unfortunately, most of us are brought up with the narrative that to get our needs met—to get approval, validation, respect, and worthiness—we must have something to show for it.

Then, we have no option but to get drawn into this battle of me vs the world. We *must* do well, *should* be better, and we *need* to come across as acceptable just so that we are loved. Thus, this quest to seek and prove takes root in childhood and continues throughout our lives until we correct the course.

I am reminded of my conversation with Sara where I asked her, 'Where is it written or who has told you that you can only be successful when you are pushing yourself, being critical, overworking, neglecting your health, and not valuing your efforts? By this logic, all successful people would be in horrible mental and physical conditions, and they wouldn't enjoy anything. But that's not what we see, is it? Can you not achieve the same destination by accepting and respecting yourself?

'What would have happened if you were nurtured with affirmations about being successful, valuable efforts, doing a good job, that it's okay to take a break, and you are enough just the way you are?'

Sara exclaimed, 'Oh my life would have been so different! I would have been more appreciative of myself, wouldn't take things personally, would be able to give myself a break and enjoy success instead of running after something else immediately.'

What if you were told different things?

I do not mean that you should overlook what is not good or not working. Instead, approach things in a way that allows you to make changes without losing your essence. View areas that need improvement—like thoughts, actions, behaviours, or habits—as opportunities for growth. Understand that the motivation for change comes from within you, recognising that you deserve better in life.

The core of self-love is acknowledging and understanding how you were not loved, understood, or validated as an individual and how that has impacted you. Then move on to work towards filling the vacuum by learning to love yourself the right way.

The truth is that most of us pass on whatever version of love is handed down to us. We do not fully grasp what we really yearn for and are on this hunt for people and avenues that can fulfil our needs and validate us. This results in poor decision-making, ignoring our inner calling, getting in and out of toxic relationships, having a poor work-life balance, and living a life that does not feel like it truly belongs to us because nothing ever feels enough. Nothing ever will until we learn to fill the gaps with self-love instead of setting limiting beliefs that make us feel nothing is enough because we were never enough.

However, does everything boil down to our childhood?

No. Not everything stems from our childhood, as we encounter various circumstances throughout our lives. Sometimes, powerful experiences in our adult life can lead to the creation of new self-limiting beliefs. When someone experiences situations such as abuse, heartbreak in relationships, setbacks or failures at work, their perception of themselves is heavily influenced. Similarly, some powerful pleasant experiences can aid in creating healthy and empowering beliefs. However, some of our deep-rooted ideas that form the core of our being and identity are influenced by our childhood. Our mind is nothing more than a pattern-forming machine; it does this to simplify existence and the process begins soon after we are born, and our mental faculties begin to take shape.

I started working with Dev about a year ago. He had been married for several years and had a 12-year-old son. Although Dev had always been a wonderful husband and father, he had been struggling with stress and anxiety for the past two years. He had retreated into his shell and did not feel like communicating with his family. Unlike his usual calm and composed self, he struggled to manage his anger. His wife had started to complain that he was never present and was always lost in his thoughts. At work, his performance had started to decline, which had begun to take a toll on him. He couldn't understand what was going on, and that's when he decided to reach out for support.

During our initial conversations, Dev shared with me that he had been feeling stressed lately due to conflicts with his parents. He explained that these conflicts had always been present, and he never really got along with his parents; he had grown accustomed to this dynamic. However, he couldn't understand why these issues were affecting him so much, especially since the stressors he was facing were unrelated to his parents directly.

As we continued to explore the underlying concerns, it became evident that Dev had always struggled with conflict resolution. He found it difficult to express his thoughts and often yielded to others' perspectives. The current stressors demanded that he confront certain people and situations, including his parents, which left him feeling anxious and preoccupied with finding the right response—a behaviour that had become habitual for him.

He harboured an innate need for his parents' approval, which intensified during conflicting situations, yet this need was never fulfilled due to his parents' emotional unavailability. His father often held opposing views on everything, while his mother remained a passive observer. Consequently, Dev grew up feeling that his thoughts and opinions were insignificant, and he developed a tendency to avoid confrontation, becoming a bystander in his own life.

Our foundational experiences during our formative years shape us, although it's not solely attributed to our parents. Interactions with others such as friends, classmates, teachers, and exposure to media also influence our beliefs and personalities. For instance, someone raised in a loving environment may still struggle due to negative experiences outside the home, such as bullying or rejection from peers and teachers.

Our subconscious absorbs information from various sources indiscriminately during childhood, forming beliefs that may persist into adulthood. As adults, we must become aware of these ingrained beliefs and thought patterns to grow and improve ourselves.

In my previous book, *The Intentional Being*, I discussed how Intention + Action = Change. One crucial intention we must set is to cultivate self-love.

Perhaps, the most important intention that we need to set is to find all this love within and give it to ourselves. I use the word 'find' because this love gets lost underneath layers of toxic behaviours and patterns that we have sustained over time. Rome was not built in a day; similarly, you wouldn't start treating yourself differently overnight. It will take time, effort, and patience. But if that's what you intend for yourself, you will get there.

All this love that you are looking for externally is right within you.

### *Exercise #3: Childhood Beliefs*

What role has your childhood played in your life?

What are some ideas, and beliefs about yourself and other aspects of your life that you have picked up? Write them down.

# 4
# FINDING LOVE WITHIN AND CHANGING THE NARRATIVE

*'One of the greatest regrets in life is being what others would want you to be, rather than being yourself.'*

**—Shannon L. Alder**

# 4.1

# Harnessing Awareness

Awareness, or even the lack of it, is a tricky space. Until we are aware of what is happening within, we continue to live on autopilot, oblivious to reality, and doing the same things repeatedly. The same is the case with our habits and beliefs. Until they operate below the level of our awareness and life seems manageable, we are at ease with the illusionary equilibrium. Many of us lead our entire lives completely unaware of why we are doing what we are doing, and it impacts our lives and relationships. All the mindless chasing and operating on autopilot continues to spread the culture of lack of self-love from one person to another. At times people can see the impact it creates on everything in their world, yet they cannot find the courage to do what is necessary to change. To separate yourself from a lack of self-love and indulge in complete self-love takes courage as it requires breaking out of your conditioning and taking on the load of disturbing the pre-existing equilibrium. It takes patience and perseverance. It is about understanding that you will be changing course and undertaking another journey that will lead you home—to your authentic self.

Me: So, Ketan, what brings you here?

Ketan: 'I have been meaning to contact you for a while, but I keep avoiding it. Then one day I just gathered the courage to . . . you know . . . reach out and see where it goes. (After a short pause he continued). I am struggling to manage my thoughts. I keep overthinking about everything. My mind is constantly thinking about something or the other. Even though I have always been like this, the past six months have been difficult. I have trouble focusing at work and my performance has started to deteriorate. This also worries me because I am working on an important project, and I cannot afford to mess that up as it's tied to the next step of my career. So, yeah, I don't know how to manage myself.'

Me: 'I hear you, Ketan, and I know that overthinking can be frustrating sometimes. I struggle with it, too, at times. However, I am curious to know a little more about the kind of thoughts you struggle with. Is there a theme that keeps running or is there a particular thing that you find yourself worrying over?

Ketan: 'Umm . . . I find myself replaying conversations in my head. The ones that have happened or at times are yet to happen. I am preoccupied with those. For instance, if I have argued with my wife, I will keep thinking about it and come up with things I could have said to her. If I have a meeting with my boss, I will think about what will happen in that meeting, what he will say, what I should do. I find it difficult to focus on what I am doing. I also get tired easily these days and struggle to sleep well. I feel like my mind is a chatterbox without a stop button!'

Me: 'That does sound a lot! Yes, it is difficult to manage so many thoughts and themes at once. You said it's always been like this, has it?'

Ketan: 'Yeah. I have always been an overthinker. I like to plan everything. I don't like being caught off guard at the last minute. I like to do things perfectly and despise making mistakes. I find conversations difficult, too. Especially if they lean towards any disagreement or conflict. I hate those.'

Me: 'I can hear the frustration in your voice. It must be very hard to keep things together, get everything right, and engage in any conversation that could lead to a disagreement or conflict.'

Ketan: 'Yes, I am constantly in my head and it's not even that I am able to say all the things that I keep thinking about. These are just random conversations that have begun to irritate me. There are times when I get so irritated that I explode!'

Me: 'Ketan, tell me if I understand this correctly, okay?'

Ketan: 'Yeah, sure.'

Me: 'From everything that you have shared so far, I have gathered that there's a lot of focus on two things—either you are worrying over things you could have said in a previous conversation, especially if there has been a disagreement or argument, or you are preparing for what's to come. If you have a meeting with your boss, and since you like to plan and prepare for everything, it's only fair for you to pre-empt what's going to happen so that you are not caught off guard. Does that resonate with you?'

Ketan (after thinking carefully): 'Yeah, that pretty much sums it all.'

Me: 'Ketan, I can also see that there is a lot of focus on planning, preparing, getting things right, not wanting to be caught off-guard. Where do you think that comes from?'

Ketan: 'Is it? I don't know . . . I have always been like this.'

Me: 'Since when?'

Ketan: 'Ever since I can remember!'

(Reflective pause)

Ketan: 'I am not sure if this is relevant, but I have always been afraid of any kind of fight or argument. It's overwhelming. When I used to see my parents fight, it would scare me a lot, and I would hide somewhere. I used to hide under my blanket as soon as I heard their voices getting louder. And then there was also this problem of sharing my opinion—it always had to be their way. I remember being scared that today I would be scolded or there would be a fight. School wasn't easy either—I was always being picked on and bullied, so I used to sit by myself and avoid other children.'

Me: 'That sounds difficult. Is that how you feel even today?'

Ketan: 'It feels like this feeling of dread never left me. It follows me like a shadow. The only way I know how to handle situations is by being prepared. If I know what's going to happen, I believe I can do something about it. I need to have control over things to prevent them from going downhill.'

Me: 'Ketan, I wonder why you drifted off into your childhood. Can you see a connection between how you feel currently and how you used to feel back then?'

Ketan: 'I think so. I feel like I am stuck in a time capsule. I have all these stories in my head that I keep replaying. Some of them are memories that randomly arise and leave me feeling exhausted because I try so hard to make them go away, but they just do not!'

Me: 'How about you drop the struggle of pushing them away and understand what they are trying to tell you?'

Ketan (snickers): 'Yeah, what choice do I have anyway?

Me: 'Well, you can continue the same way . . .'

Ketan: 'No, I don't want to. I cannot. I am tired. I need better ways to handle things otherwise everything will become a mess.'

Me: 'You know, awareness is the first step towards change, and you have already taken that. Now you need to keep going in the direction that you want to.'

Ketan: 'Will I be able to get out of this?'

Me: 'Do you want to?'

Ketan: 'Yes, of course!'

Me: 'Then you will. It might take some time to unpack your inner world to understand what's happening and what needs to change, but you will get there.'

Most of our narratives stem from our experiences that serve as supporting evidence to keep that narrative going. For instance, I believe I am an incompetent driver. This idea was formed after my repeated failures with driving. Now, even if I try to drive, my mind involuntarily rejects the idea. Negative thoughts start cropping up, which create a lot of discomfort and anxiety around driving, making sure I am not in the right state to drive even if the need arises. My mind has created this narrative around my driving abilities based on my experiences, and if I had a different set of experiences, my narrative would have been different. Essentially, all these narratives are our creations. They help us create a sense of identity as we learn to find our voice and place in the world. There is nothing absolute about them because we are all viewing the world with our unique lenses.

For the longest time, I believed that my parents loved my brother more than me. There were certainly incidents and events where he was given preference over me, but there were also instances where that did not happen. In all these years, both types of events have occurred, and I have always found it hard to believe anything else other than my belief. I found reasons to negate contrary evidence because my beliefs would always get the better of me. Underneath this idea was my core belief that 'I am not good enough', 'I am a disappointment', and 'I am useless' so why would they love me? Of course, they would love him more because he was better than me.

As time passed, I realised that there were a lot of experiences that served as genuine evidence for some of my self-limiting beliefs to take shape. However, there were also times when I had created a perspective around my own beliefs on autopilot. When I received a gold medal in my master's degree, I should have been ecstatic. For someone who had only received a certificate of complete attendance in school, I should have been over the moon. But I was not. I tossed the feelings of happiness aside as if it were not a big deal. I never talked about it, and I asked my friends not to tell anyone. I came home from my convocation and stuffed it in the back of some cupboard because I believed that I was not good enough and my efforts did not matter. Even though everyone around me was singing praises, I was not confident in my abilities.

My ideas about myself were not just limited to subtle behaviours. I had started talking about myself in the worst way possible. My friends would often ask me, 'Why are you so pessimistic about yourself?' I had no answer except for, 'I am just like this.'

The point is that I was the one who kept this narrative going, blissfully unaware of my actions. I looked at all my limitations as a final character judgment. The more I engaged in this thought pattern, the more I was pulled into it. However, this changed when I focused inward. I first had to become aware of my narratives and their patterns. I had to harness self-awareness and become conscious every time the narrative showed up and learn new skills and strategies to get off the autopilot.

When I faced any setback or failure in life, I had to learn to repeat that it was a learning experience and there's always a next time instead of giving up.

We are all a work in progress. There is no perfection and no end to human evolution. Our job as humans is to continue to grow and evolve into different versions of ourselves. We get to choose those versions. Yes, life will get in the way, we may not get everything we want, and there will always be something out of our control, but we will have the ability to control our thoughts, emotions, and actions. Our purpose is to focus on these so that we can create a well-rounded and meaningful life that not only looks good on the outside but feels good on the inside as well. It all starts with understanding the narrative that we have built around ourselves and our world.

## 4.2
## Understanding the Narrative

We are all storytellers in our own right. Our world is made of stories that we hear from others and those we write ourselves. This is a primary way to find some meaning in this chaotic world.

According to Dr Stephen Madigan, author of the bestselling book, *Narrative Therapy*, 'The concept of identity is cultural, discursive, multisided, multi-storied, contextual, and relational. Our narratives are dynamic and built concerning the shifting identities in various contexts. It is the interpretation of these narratives that is central to our identity and shapes the way we think, feel, and behave. It is the narratives and the interpretations of those that contribute to our overall well-being and the way we find our place in the world.'

We all come up with some or the other narrative to keep us going. Sometimes it is helpful and empowering, and sometimes it is not. But not all unhelpful narratives need to be changed. There is merit in every kind of narrative that we build and live by because they all play a crucial role in forming our identity in different ways. However, a story, narrative, or interpretation becomes problematic when it begins to reduce the overall quality of our lives instead of adding value to it. Every time that story or narrative starts to play, it disturbs you emotionally, creates difficulty in your day-to-day functioning, disrupts your relationships, and takes a toll on your overall health and well-being. This means that your narrative is problem-saturated, indicating that you have begun to overidentify with the narrative and perceive yourself as the problem.

For instance, if your ideas about yourself include statements like 'I am not good enough' or 'Not capable enough' or 'I am unworthy' or 'I don't deserve anything good' or 'Nothing good ever happens to me' or 'Life is unfair' or 'Relationships are difficult' or 'Money does not come easily to me' or 'I can never be successful' or 'No one loves me' or 'I have to look a certain way to be accepted' and have taken over different aspects of your life, it is time to hit pause and understand what needs to change.

When Rahul came to me for a session, he was clear about his issues. He said, 'There is no problem in my life. I am the problem. Everything is going well. I have a stable career, a good married life, and a social circle. Yet, I find myself being reactive at times. I get annoyed at the smallest of things and have this nagging thought that nobody loves me. This makes me insecure, and I ask my wife for reassurance repeatedly. Initially, she used to be understanding and patient with me. But I think it's starting to get to her now. Sometimes, I find feel quite low and lost along with feeling disconnected from everything.'

When I asked him whether the thought 'nobody loves me' had recently come to his awareness or had been there for a long time, he said that he had always felt this about himself. Rahul had always believed that he was unlovable, no one liked or loved him owing to certain events that he had experienced in life. He never needed to change or do something about it because things were fine. Only when this narrative had started to disrupt the flow of his life did he pay attention to some persistent stories and interpretations that arose and decided to do something about them?

Thus, it is important to become aware of what you are constantly telling yourself because thoughts turn into stories and those stories define your reality. The most problematic stories are the ones where we become the problem and take that to be the truth. This distorts the way we perceive ourselves and become hyper focused on our supposed flaws and shortcomings. Instead of considering other important factors in our lives, we only focus on one problem: I, me, and myself. Viewing yourself as the problem all the time is disempowering.

We create stories and interpretations about everything, especially ourselves. Then why not create the ones that are uplifting and empowering? To do so, we must become aware of the current narrative that is keeping us from loving ourselves. Explore why it needs to change and what we will gain once we change this narrative. This reflection is crucial because until we feel that the stories and beliefs, we are operating from are serving us, we wouldn't want to change them.

Another important thing to understand about changing the narrative is—it was, is, and will always be about you. Others are the only side characters in your story; you are the hero. You need to consciously pull yourself out of the 'should' cycle. When it comes to changing our life story, we often equate it to trying to make others understand what they have done wrong, what they should be doing instead, and so on.

Yes, your life would have been different only if your parents, siblings, and others were different or could have done things differently. But the fact is that they did what they could, and they will continue to do what they can. Focusing on trying to change them, especially when they are unwilling and incapable of changing, will only lead to misery.

Moreover, whatever happened in the past that played an important role in shaping your narrative about yourself has already passed. You cannot go back in time to undo anything; you can only move forward. Your experiences and emotions were, are, and will always be valid. However, holding onto the past will not let you live in the present and take away what you have now. To create a better future, you need to change the narrative about yourself that is keeping you from loving yourself.

*If you can find a way to survive amidst all the chaos, imagine what you will be able to create with the awareness and choice you have now.*

Perhaps, the most important aspect we tend to overlook is the element of choice. We have complete authority over our individual choices—not making a choice is also a choice. Instead of wishful thinking, we need to engage in purposeful thinking in the present. We must operate with knowledge and awareness to make better choices now. Otherwise, after a few years, we will sit with regret and wonder, 'Only if I had done things differently, then . . .' Thus, the time to change the narrative is now.

### *Exercise #4: What's Your Current Story?*

a. What are some of the self-limiting beliefs you have about yourself?

I am/I have to/I am not/I cannot:

b. What is the impact of continuing to live with these ideas in the following areas of your life?

Relationships:

Work:

Health:

Dreams and Visions for the Future:

c. What has contributed to the development of these self-limiting ideas?

d. What are some ways in which you reinforce these ideas?

## 4.3

## Acknowledging Resistance

An important thing to remember while working with your internal narrative is that even when you are aware of it and are willing to change it, it will not happen overnight. These stories, ideas, and beliefs that surround you and define your identity, require patience and persistent effort to crack. As your current narrative is conditioned into your mind over the years, change will also take place gradually. An essential component that needs attention and understanding here is resistance.

Sometimes when we know something needs to change and why, we may still struggle to take the necessary steps to start. That's because our mind loves to be in its comfort zone. It works on only two principles—pleasure and pain. This pleasure-pain principle was first identified by the prominent psychologist Sigmund Freud. He argued that we either move towards people, places, events, and situations that give us pleasure or away from the ones that give us pain, psychologically or emotionally. This is a part of our basic survival mechanism; we tend to gravitate towards instant gratification. This means that our mind will create habits and patterns of certain repeated thoughts and behaviours so that we do not have to keep spending time and energy going over them again and again. Once a habit is formed, it can be placed into an automatic mode. It frees up more mental, emotional, and physical energy for the next thought or behaviour a situation demands.

This is why, even when we know that certain thoughts, reactions, behaviours, or habits are detrimental to us, we continue to engage with them because of comfort. The mind resists making any new changes, fearing the loss of that comfort zone. For instance, you know that you must wake up on time to hit the gym because you want to work on your fitness goals. Yet, you struggle to wake up and hit the snooze button multiple times before waking up, only to fall back asleep.

If breaking out of old habits and setting new ones can prove to be challenging, imagine how difficult it is to change a belief or narrative that has defined your identity as a person. Hence, it is crucial to change these narratives to find the love you have within yourself as a journey.

Till now, you had a readymade narrative about yourself, which enabled you to fulfil your needs by engaging in certain behaviours. However, if you still feel disconnected from yourself or find your existing narrative depleting the quality of your life, you need to weigh its short-term and long-term gains.

After a few sessions, Mira had an important decision to make. But before that, she had some questions.

Mira: 'I was thinking about our conversation the other day, the fact that I love myself conditionally. I think you were right.'

Me: 'Hmm. And how did you arrive at this conclusion?'

Mira: 'I mean I still haven't grasped it completely, but I am beginning to see that I like myself for certain things and am uncomfortable with myself in other areas. There's also a constant feeling of not being able to fit in anywhere—whether it's family or in my friends' circle—I am the oddball trying to be someone so that I can be perceived in a certain way.'

Me: 'And what way is that?'

Mira: 'Someone who belongs . . . I never felt I did. Sometimes, it was because of my weight or my being less 'girly'. I feel like I am under this pressure to be perfect all the time. At times I want to let my hair down, but I cannot do so. I have worked hard to create this image of a person who is put together and has everything under control, but I don't feel that way. I keep thinking that I need to do more and more because what I am doing does not feel enough. But then this is all I know. At least I have friends, I am doing well in my studies, and I am fulfilling expectations. What else do I do if not this?'

Me: 'I hear you, Mira, and I understand where you are coming from. You have built yourself in a certain manner that has served you in so many ways. I also see your internal dilemma to continue this or explore another way of being. Would you be open to exploring this a bit more?'

Mira: 'Sure.'

Me: 'Tell me, this current narrative that you have, how is it benefiting you?'

Mira: 'I think, it's largely not. I feel like I am always wearing a mask and trying to prove to people or get them to acknowledge me or consider me in some way. But at the end of the day, I am still not happy. I am conscious of what people think of me, whether I am being judged or not, if my friends would leave me or not. Now, I don't even want to lose weight! I know it's important for me, but I am scared—what if I lose weight and people still don't like me?'

Me: 'I hear you. So, if you can see that it's getting a bit difficult to keep up, is there another way that you would like to be with yourself? Perhaps, create a different narrative about yourself that would be a bit easier to keep up with? Or something that makes you happy?'

Mira (after some moments of reflection): 'Yes. I think I just want to believe that I am good enough and worthy of all the good things. Like you had said, I cannot keep running after people's opinions. I mean, I do that already and it stops me from overthinking. I guess I would like to be content with who I am. Self-love seems unrealistic to me right now, but I would like to get there.'

Me: 'And what would become possible for you if you were to believe that you are good enough?'

Mira: 'So much! I wouldn't be worried about others' opinions; I will be able to do what I want and enjoy everything. I will be able to let my hair down, and if I don't feel like doing something or going somewhere, then I will say exactly that. I will feel like myself.'

The key to overcoming this resistance from your comfort zone is to create a new story that brings lasting satisfaction. Your mind may struggle to let go of the old narrative, but it's important to keep reminding yourself of what lies ahead. Just because something feels comfortable now does not mean it will remain that way.

Drawing from the pain-pleasure principle, the focus is on creating a new narrative that enables you to feel good and empowered.

***Exercise #5: Create Your New Narrative***

Write down:

- What new narrative do you want to create?

____________________________________________

____________________________________________

____________________________________________

____________________________________________

____________________________________________

____________________________________________

____________________________________________

____________________________________________

____________________________________________

____________________________________________

____________________________________________

____________________________________________

- What is the new belief that you want to strengthen about yourself?

  Begin with: 'I am . . .'

____________________________________________

____________________________________________

____________________________________________

____________________________________________

____________________________________________

____________________________________________

____________________________________________

____________________________________________

- What will become possible for you because of this new narrative?

# 5
# THE POWER OF CHANGING YOUR NARRATIVE

*'You are the storyteller of your own life, and you can create your own legend or not.'*

**—Isabel Allende**

## 5.1
## Stories of Self-Love

Here are snippets of some people who decided to change their narrative and embrace self-love. Each one of them faced unique challenges and life circumstances. Their journey was not easy as they had to unlearn and relearn a lot while making changes within. At the end of the day, no matter where they are in their journey, they are at ease with themselves and continue to harness love in its entirety.

***Disha, 25***

As I write this, I feel proud of the fact that I have come so far in my life. Since childhood I was never taught how to love myself, nor did I have any idea about it. What I felt was the presence of a problem within. I was never taught to appreciate the steps I was taking, instead, I was always compared to what others were doing.

I struggled to accept myself. Being a thin girl was always a problem for the people around me—I was never accepted the way I was and being constantly compared to others made me feel helpless. Being good at academics was the only way through as I felt appreciated and accepted. I was unable to see myself for who I was; I started criticising myself when things went wrong. I always wanted to do things perfectly to prove my worth to others, even when I had no control over the task at hand. I did not want to make any mistakes as I feared being judged. My entire childhood and school life made it difficult for me to love myself. I started being hard on myself for everything and believed that being a teenager was a problem or I was the problem. In all my relationships since childhood, I was reinforcing the belief that I was not enough. Perfectionism seemed to be the only viable way to be loved.

Eventually, I couldn't handle this and desired self-love more than ever. I gradually started my healing process, giving myself plenty of time. I accepted my flaws, and the reasons behind them, and began seeing myself for who I was. When you start healing and prioritise yourself, it brings you closer to your feelings. Addressing, accepting, and allowing yourself to be yourself makes all the difference.

I could never stand up for myself in the past, however, now I can love myself for who I am even on the days I make mistakes. I am sensitive to my feelings, and I do not allow anybody the power to dictate my feelings. I am now my top priority and I love myself. I feel I am in a better place with myself than I have ever been—I accept my body with all its flaws, I love myself without conditions, I love who I am right now, and I cannot be any less grateful for it.

***A. Sethi, 19***

For as long as I can remember, I have struggled to fit into the mould the world had set for me. I was not working hard enough, motivated enough, or meeting the expectations of a world indifferent to the inner turmoil I was experiencing. Far from self-love, I couldn't even fathom acknowledging myself—that who I was not the illusory, perfect person the world told me I should be. I was running from the world, myself, and overbearing pressure. A year ago, my legs finally gave out. Wallowing in self-pity and drowning in the darkness that enveloped me, I wept and cried to anyone who would listen, except my family, lest they know the truth behind the increasingly onerous smile. The mind has a nasty manner of seeking the worst in oneself—it reviewed the evidence and held me guilty of inflicting my pain onto my audience by the sinister act of speaking about it. This started a vicious cycle of weeping, calling someone, and sobbing ever harder for contacting them at all. Around then, I was pushed to seek professional help, and I have forever been grateful for that.

With a mixture of medication and the incredibly patient support of my therapist, I started to rise from the depths of my despair. I learnt, slowly but surely, to accept myself in all my flawed glory. It turns out it is okay not to follow the template but to follow your unique, messy, often circular trajectory to being who you are. For better or worse, I began to accept that what worked for me was not necessarily what the world wanted and that it was entirely okay for that to be the case.

As simple as it sounds, it took me months to realise the power of this sentence—the magical ability to make me comfortable in my skin, to make the previously foreign concept of self-love comprehensible. It is still an uphill journey each day to accept myself for who I am; however, the slope is much easier to overcome now with practise and patience.

It is an integral part of love to allow failures and, as such, to allow yourself to fail without getting lost in the despair of blame. I will forever be grateful for the people who have supported me in this journey, which has been interesting thus far, and I hope it's far from over.

### *Reema, 45*

Coming from a humble family, I placed importance on work and financial stability. I was succeeding as a professional and experiencing financial success and career stability. Even after being diagnosed with stage IV breast cancer, I remained resilient and managed well with the treatment. However, there were moments when I found myself at rock bottom, vulnerable, and on the brink of tears, making me furious. I had to endure several sleepless nights. I struggled to manage my emotional state, which was affecting me mentally and manifesting as physical ailments. It was then that I decided to seek professional help.

With the help of my therapist, I was able to uncover the different facets of my life that had impacted me a lot. My childhood was challenging, marked by hard work, violence, fear, and threats. The concept of self-love was expressed solely through perfection, work, discipline, and achieving success. All notions of self-love—respect, happiness, joy, and responsibility were distorted by the instinct of survival mode that developed during my childhood.

As I started focusing on my internal world, I gained more insight into my mental and emotional state. I was able to achieve small victories, such as calmly managing client meetings and maintaining a positive demeanour, as opposed to being angry and upset afterwards. I also established genuine communication with my daughter, fostering a harmonious connection that lasted for months, versus the frequent conflicts and silence we were experiencing before. I reclaimed restful sleep and enhanced my self-love. I am now capable of savouring self-love and embracing life.

Can you see what these stories have in common? All of them have their own life stories, traumas, and roadblocks. They grew up with a belief system about themselves that was not healthy or conducive to their growth and reached a point where they knew something needed to change. It took them time, effort, patience, and persistence. It also took me all of this and more to be able to say, 'I am okay'. I know that if you are struggling with yourself, you can get there, too.

It does not matter where we come from; what matters is where we want to go. If you want to love yourself more, all you need to do is find a new way of looking at yourself and allow yourself time to let it sink in.

# 6
# CULTIVATING SELF-LOVE

*'We are each gifted in a unique and important way. It is our privilege and our adventure to discover our own special light.'*

**—Mary Dunbar**

## 6.1

## Nurturing Childhood Gaps

Childhood is a vulnerable space. When a child arrives in this world, wailing and screaming, they need to be held and assured that regardless of what happens someone will be there to take care of and protect them. The sense of safety and security provided by the primary caregivers builds the foundation on which the child develops their identity.

John Bowlby, in his theory of attachment, postulated that bonding and attachment are innate human needs that are hardwired in us. For a child to grow and develop into a secure individual, they need a predictable physical and emotional connection with an attachment figure, such as parents, siblings, and friends. This connection can calm the nervous system and provide a safe haven where comfort and reassurance can be reliably obtained, allowing for emotional balance to be maintained and restored when needed. This dependency on a loved one during the child's formative years creates a secure base, giving the child a platform from which they can slowly move into the world, take risks, explore, and develop a sense of autonomy while feeling reassured, taken care of, loved, and supported. The mere presence—physical and emotional—and responsiveness of the caregiver or attachment figure(s) acts as the primary sources for the identity and belief formation of the child. Perhaps, the only question a child needs answered at every step while growing up is 'Are you there for me?' in every sense. An affirmative response to this question creates the feelings of being seen, heard, accepted, validated, and loved. But what happens when, in subtle or sometimes obvious ways, you experience the absence of your caregivers or attachment figures? In this case, a vacuum begins to set in, one that is filled with the existential question, 'Do I even matter?' 'Am I important?' 'Am I not good enough or worthy of being loved?'

In reality, there is nothing else that a child is capable of thinking because they do not have the logical, mature filters to make sense of this confusing, chaotic adult world where there can be numerous reasons and circumstances leading to a particular behaviour of adults. At times, there is an obvious and blatant denial, neglect, and ignorance of a child's emotional, psychological, and physical needs. At other times, it may be subtle or unintended. But for the child, there is no other explanation other than 'something must be wrong with me, that's why I am not being loved and accepted' that makes sense.

However, as adults, we need to understand that we do have those filters and now it is up to us to recognise the gaps that our own upbringing, life stories, and circumstances have created in our narratives and fill them up on our own. We need to do this not because this is something that we must, but because we can. Thus, coming home to yourself is about returning to your roots that say, 'I am good enough and capable of more,' which requires a blend of some crucial skills and concepts.

**Concept #1: Learning to Affirm Yourself**

It is incredibly difficult to love yourself when you have grown up feeling unseen, unheard, and invalidated; your major driving

force being a vacuum stemming from emotional deprivation. This emotional deprivation makes you feel unworthy, forcing you to settle for a life that is inauthentic and disconnected from who you truly are. Unfortunately, this deprivation is a result of how society propagates certain ways of being. Regardless of what we do, something about us will always be 'not good enough'. Only if someone was tall enough, slim enough, plump enough, qualified enough, rich enough, successful enough—the list is endless—maybe then we would be 'good enough' and worthy of something.

But what is enough? Over time, nothing feels enough because we do not have a concept of 'enough'. I remember discussing this with a client who said he wanted to reach a space where he could feel he had a stable ground to stand on. He felt that he lacked a strong foundation because nothing was ever enough, and this is something we must do for ourselves—we need to be able to have a sturdy foundation of self-beliefs to stand on, to be able to tell ourselves: 'I am enough' instead of shredding ourselves to pieces. Being enough is not the end; it is the beginning of the exploration of the infinite potential that you have within yourself. It is the solid ground on which you build yourself and move towards being your authentic self.

Being enough gives you the ability and power to be more of who you already are instead of being a version that is disconnected from your true spirit. The fundamental question is not what you need to 'do' to be validated or feel that you matter; it's about how you can be more of yourself.

Then, the entire journey of loving yourself becomes about one important concept—self-affirmation.

Being able to affirm yourself means being present with yourself, giving your full attention to understand your inner world, including thoughts, emotions, needs, desires, and behaviours that constitute it. As Conrad Baars wrote in his book *Healing the Unaffirmed*, 'The concept of affirmation is much more complex than it seems at first glance. It is not something that a person does to another. Rather, it is a state of being, of being aware and being moved by the goodness of another being. Authentic affirmation is never a technique aimed at changing the will or conditioning the mind. It is a way of being present to another individual with the full attention of one's whole being.'

Concisely, it means that for a child to develop to its full potential, its presence needs to be affirmed by the caretakers and the world around it. Children must feel that someone is genuinely concerned about them and their psychological and emotional experiences to be able to step out into the world and gradually become independent. It's only then that this void of dependency is filled. However, since most of us are oblivious to understanding this affirmation, we grow up with a void that becomes hard to fill.

We need people around us to be wholeheartedly present for us during our formative years. We need to know that our thoughts, emotions, and experiences matter, and someone will be there to hold space for us, hear us out, and help us make sense of the world. When we lack this kind of presence, we grow up with certain gaps in our thinking and beliefs. These gaps push us into survival mode, where we start operating under the premise of, 'What do I do to make my presence felt?' This further leads us to adopt certain habits and behaviours that divert our attention and energy away from ourselves. Eventually, we reach a point where the sense of deprivation and vacuum begins to gnaw at us, and we feel that trying hard to be seen and valued is pointless. As a result, we end up feeling even more invisible.

When this realisation sets in, it's time to turn our attention inwards and reverse the process, meaning, it's time to come home to the fact that as a fully functional adult, our journey is about four fundamental concepts.

**Concept #2: Recognising Your Unmet Needs**

To survive in the physical world, we need to fulfil our physical needs; to thrive in the emotional world, we need to meet our emotional needs.

According to American psychologist Marshall Rosenberg, founder of the Nonviolent Communication model, 'Needs are universal values that drive all our actions as human beings. They include anything that a person needs to sustain life no matter their race, religious preference, financial status, location, or culture. Needs then are the basic things all people need to support life. We often think of needs as food, air, and water. Those are certainly needed for our survival, and we also need so much more to thrive and be fully alive.'

When we understand that our behaviours are attempts to meet certain needs, we become more adept at choosing behaviours that will help us meet those needs in a healthier manner; thus, enabling us to lead a fuller life. This process begins from the moment we enter this world. However, we cannot fulfil those needs in isolation; we need to connect with one another.

When we grow up in environments where our needs of safety, security, and attachment are met to a sufficient degree, we navigate through life with a sense of security and ease. However, when this does not happen, owing to various reasons such as parental neglect, inconsistent parenting, emotional or physical abuse, trauma, conflicted family dynamics, or any other social or environmental factors, it leads to a disconnect with the self, impaired mind-body connection, psychological, emotional, interpersonal difficulties, and disturbances. With time we get caught up in various strategies to meet those needs that extract a huge cost. That's why we often hear people say, 'I do so much for people and get nothing in return.' Such individuals perpetually live in a state of dysfunction, unhappiness, and misery.

A huge part of changing your narrative relies on recognising your unmet needs, which is essentially about unlearning old strategies and replacing them with new, healthier ones. This is crucial because when we come from a place of vacuum and deprivation—even if things are different in the present—our mind continues to look at everything from the lens of that vacuum. We keep doubting the value of ourselves, our relationships, and our work. The more we continue to chase, the more elusive those needs become. Over time, the vacuum becomes a home to various existential fears that are incredibly hard to navigate. We fear abandonment, rejection, failure, and loneliness. Without awareness of our fundamental needs and constructive strategies to meet them, we often find ourselves trapped in cycles of dysfunction.

Neha: 'I am stuck.'

Me: 'Go on, I am listening.'

Neha: 'You know the boy I told you about?'

Me: 'Umm, the one you started dating a few months ago?'

Neha: 'Yes. We have been together for a few months now. Everything was fine in the beginning, but lately, things have been difficult.'

Me: 'Tell me more.'

Neha: 'He keeps lashing out at me for the smallest of things, constantly berating me. Sometimes I am the stupidest girl on this earth, or I am fat. If I do not do what he wants me to do, the arguments turn insane. I try to make him understand but he does not listen. The other day he created a huge scene on the road, leaving me mortified. I did not know what to do, so I cried. I feel so helpless and lost; I have lost confidence in myself. Sometimes, I feel like ending this relationship, but I cannot bring myself to do that. Just the thought of it scares the daylights out of me!'

Me: 'I hear you, Neha, and I can see that you are in a lot of distress. Can you share a bit more about this fear?'

Neha: 'A part of me says that I should leave him, however, the minute this thought crops up, I become anxious and think about how I will live. He is all I have right now, and I have never really had anyone. If he is not there either, I'll be all alone . . . I do not want to be alone. I have always thought myself to be unlovable. So, when we have some good days, everything feels all right, and all the terrible things seem to be mere imagination.'

Me: 'Are you really imagining those things?'

Neha: 'No. His behaviour is making it difficult for me to believe that it's all in my head. Everyone has been telling me to get out of this relationship, but I am stuck.'

It was important for Neha to unpack her fear of being alone and get in touch with her needs for safety, connection, understanding, acceptance, and respect to evaluate her relationship. This is something we all need to do occasionally. A key component of loving yourself is identifying your core needs and what would fulfil them, enabling you to choose behaviours, opportunities, and people that support optimal fulfilment. Most importantly, before seeking validation from others, we must learn to meet these needs ourselves. For example, if you desire respect from others, begin by respecting yourself. If you seek acceptance and appreciation, start by accepting and appreciating yourself.

*Being cognisant of your needs and supporting yourself is essential because when you get caught up in situations where you feel unfulfilled, you know that your needs are your responsibility. If someone or something doesn't meet them, you do not disintegrate; instead, you recognise and take action.* Remember, these are *your* needs. Thus, they are and will always be your responsibility. People, places, and events are only a means for fulfilment, but you are the source. The way you treat yourself is how you tell the world to treat you. We need to remember that, as adults, we can make choices and harness our power to change things. Yes, our baggage of unfulfillment will weigh us down, making it difficult for us to move forward, but it's not impossible. This is the only thing we need to do to be able to change those dysfunctional narratives and heal.

It is about asking yourself: 'What do I need from the various aspects of my life to feel fulfilled?'

### *Exercise #6: Recognising Needs*

a. What were some of your needs that were not met while growing up?
b. What would you have wanted your parents/caretakers to have done differently?

**Needs Checklist**

Being aware of our core needs enables us to create a more stable, fulfilling life. Below is a list of universal needs; however, they may differ from one individual to another based on their importance. Additionally, our needs may also change with time and life circumstances.

Read the list and identify your top ten core needs that you want your life goals and relationships to fulfil for you:

- Communication
- Safety
- Security
- Stability
- Support
- To feel seen
- To be heard
- To be understood
- Trust
- Warmth
- Friendship
- Inclusion
- Intimacy
- Independence
- Connection
- Affection
- Appreciation
- Acceptance
- Co-operation
- Companionship
- Consideration
- Empathy
- Consistency
- Respect
- Nurturing
- To understand
- Community
- Compassion

- Freedom
- Space
- Clarity
- Growth
- Learning
- Self-expression
- Awareness
- Celebration
- Challenge
- Creativity
- Closeness
- Stimulation
- Self-respect
- Honesty
- Authenticity
- Joy
- Humour
- Peace
- Equality
- Harmony
- Love
- Achievement
- Choice
- Belonging
- Integrity
- Fun

### Concept #3: Being Present for Yourself

I matter—these two words are the crux of self-love. Instead of spending all your time and energy negating your emotional experiences or looking for an external lens to validate them, learn to open yourself up to them. It involves sitting with your vulnerable parts, engaging in a conversation with them, and telling them: 'I hear you,' 'I feel you,' and 'I am there for you.'.

When our needs are not met, we slowly start to lose parts of ourselves. The parts that were supposed to shine, go into oblivion and only those that enable us to survive take control. Eventually, we become invisible not only to others but also to ourselves. Here, the need for self-preservation kicks in. On this self-love journey, you need to learn to say, 'I am here for myself,' and build on this foundation by recognising your importance, value, and worthiness because you exist. It is also about creating a strong internal narrative that revolves around the belief of being good enough and capable of much more and that your presence matters to you. For some of us, this may be unfathomable because we have believed that our presence or absence does not matter; however, that is a narrative that helped you survive—your need for self-preservation made you look at yourself a certain way. A part of you already considered yourself important.

By being present to yourself, you can move to a healthier narrative that does not stop at survival, instead, it lets you thrive.

Ketan (excitedly): 'I want to tell you something!'

Me: 'Sure, go ahead!'

Ketan: 'So, last week I told you I had been avoiding some friends for a long time, right?'

Me: 'Yes, I remember.'

Ketan: 'I was avoiding them because they had not treated me well, and as I usually avoid all sorts of confrontations or disagreements, I thought it was best to avoid it this time as well. I thought, "What if I say something and they do not understand or agree, it will then become awkward for me." But last week, when one of my friends reached out to plan, I gathered some courage to tell him how I felt uncomfortable with certain things, and if they want to hang out with me, they will have to consider them.'

Me: 'Wow! I am glad that you took this step. I know it must have been challenging, but you did it anyway.'

Ketan: 'Oh, yes! I was so anxious that I must have replayed the conversation a thousand times in my head before actually saying it. Even during the conversation, my heart was racing. However, I felt a huge sense of relief.'

Me: 'Yes, that relief is apparent in your demeanour today. Your conversation is a lot smoother, and your body is relaxed.'

Ketan: 'Yeah, I feel like a load has been lifted off me.'

Me: 'And what prompted you to take this step?'

Ketan: 'Well, firstly I am beginning to understand the areas where I need to change and that I will always want to run away because that is what I do. So, I must start somewhere. This seemed a bit easier than the other areas where I am struggling now, so I thought I would take the risk. I have noticed that a faint voice in my head reminds me that I am important, too, and my feelings matter. I want to strengthen it.'

Me: 'That's wonderful, Ketan. Tell me, how are you feeling this?'

Ketan: 'Relieved, of course! I feel like I am moving in the right direction. I know talking to my wife or parents would be much harder, but it seems possible. I know their perspective is important and I want to balance it by giving importance to my own as well.'

**Concept #4: Re-Parenting Yourself**

Canadian psychiatrist Eric Berne first propounded the concept of re-parenting as a part of the therapeutic approach known as Transactional Analysis. It involves understanding those childhood needs that were initially unfulfilled and then working towards their fulfilment. Reparenting yourself enables you to look at the needs that were not met, recognise the impact of your childhood experiences on your development as an individual, and change the negative scripts that you hold about yourself into a better and more attuned version of who you are and who you would like to be.

In a nutshell, it is about learning to give yourself the kind of attention, understanding, acceptance, and love that you did not receive growing up; supporting yourself in ways you always wanted someone else to and tapping into your power. It is also about building yourself from the ground up by laying foundations on your own with full ownership. Affirming and re-parenting yourself are intricately connected. When you can get into the mindset of being present to your experiences, you can tap into your unmet needs and dysfunctional behaviours, finding healthier ways of meeting your needs as an adult.

Parenting yourself is challenging and, in several ways, it defies the concept of traditional parenting. We rely on our parents to perform this complex task of parenting for us, rather than trying to parent ourselves. As complex as it may seem, it is necessary because we cannot let the coping mechanisms we used as children run our world as adults. Reparenting ourselves means shedding the years of conditioning and layers of beliefs that surround our spirit. Here, we will have to dismantle our ideas about everything and build something new.

A conditioned vacuum can be generational. If our parents were never affirmed as children, they grow up to be individuals who do the same and pass their vacuum down to us. However, once we enter adulthood and reach a point where those teachings are not working in our favour, it is our responsibility to give birth to a new belief system and an identity we want to create. It is a long road ahead of us filled with ups and downs.

However, at the end of the day, if you can feel complete from within and look in the mirror, telling yourself, 'I am important,' 'I matter,' 'I am enough,' and 'I am worthy' with a sense of peace and fulfilment, the struggle is worthwhile. What lies at the end of this long road is a healed version of yourself—one that understands its desires, and needs, and is mature enough to nurture the inner child. This version fearlessly presents itself to the world, claiming its rightful space and love.

**Concept #5: Setting an Intention**

The only way to change your narrative and love yourself the right way is through setting an intention for yourself—consciously choosing where and how you would like to invest your mental, emotional, and physical energy to create the kind of life you want.

We are mostly on autopilot, doing things because we are used to them or because that is how they are supposed to be done. Eventually, we get stuck in this rut of doing more without realising whether it works for us. Being intentional with yourself is about learning to hit pause to step back and look at what you are doing, why you are doing it, and what you would like to do instead. As I wrote in my previous book, *The Intentional Being*, 'When you start defining where you would like to put your energies and how, you begin to create shifts within yourself and in your life. You are able to find joy, satisfaction, ease, meaning and contentment in everything that you do.' Your action plans and goals are the means to fulfil your intention of being or feeling a certain way.

Setting an intention for yourself lets you get into certain mental states wherein you can focus on changing those specific thought patterns, emotional responses, and behaviours that enable you to become a better, more fulfilled version of yourself.

Supposedly, if you want to go on a vacation, you first need to decide the destination. Once you have clarity about your destination, you can create an action plan that will help you get there. Thus, your intention is your roadmap for the kind of person you want to become and the life you want to live. Intention combined with purposeful action results in meaningful changes in every area of your life—both being equally important because intention without action is only wishful thinking. Similarly, if we engage in actions without being intentional about their purpose, we will always be running around like headless chickens.

Hence, to be able to create meaningful shifts, you need to ask yourself the following questions:

1. What kind of a person do I want to be?
2. What kind of a life do I want to lead?
3. How do I want to feel about myself?

Once we become conscious of our internal processes in one area of our lives and make meaningful changes, our minds can transfer those lessons to other areas as well. However, does this mean all of life's problems will vanish and that people will change to be the way you want them to be? Absolutely not.

Being intentional with yourself and your life means focusing more on what you can control and change, rather than grappling with the uncontrollable variables of life. It allows you to feel more in touch with choices that align with your values, rather than being at the mercy of other people and situations. It is about embracing the new narrative that you have created for yourself and aligning everything with it.

For instance, if you say you intend to be healthy, you will have to make necessary changes in your lifestyle. You will have to choose exercises that suit you, figure out a nutrition plan, and sleep well. Regardless of how big or small the change may be, you will have to do what you think is doable and fosters improvement. Not everyone likes to go to the gym, nor does everyone like adhering to a strict diet plan. However, you will be able to make a decision that suits you once you are sure about your intention and the possible steps required to fulfil it.

The same principle applies to loving yourself—you first need to establish your definition and understanding of self-love and then engage in habits and behaviours that fit that definition. Regardless of life's challenges, you must build a solid foundation that will let you nurture and support yourself, empowering you to move forward with self-love. Thus, to truly love yourself, you need to set an intention for yourself so that your mind can start moving in that direction and pick up ways of thinking and behaving that feel more aligned with your values.

To create your intention, here are some things to keep in mind:

- Your intention needs to be clear and precise—it needs to be positively worded
- You need to focus on what you want and how you want to feel instead of thinking about what you do not want or do not want to feel
- Keep the action steps simple and realistic
- Elaborate on how you want to feel in different areas of your life

Remember, your intention for yourself will set the tone for ways you show up for yourself.

### *Exercise #7: What's Your Intention for Yourself?*

a. How do you want to show up for yourself from now on?

b. What are some of the ideas that you want to strengthen about yourself? How will you feel by doing so?

c. How different would your life be if you started showing up for yourself differently?

Complete: 'From now on I am going to . . .'

## 6.2

# Opening the Doors to Your Inner Child

I wish I could tell you there is a magic formula to love yourself or a quick fix that will change the way you perceive yourself overnight. I wish I could tell you that all you need to do is apply a bunch of techniques and see the results within a few days or weeks. The truth is there is no shortcut to self-love.

No formula will undo everything that you have come to believe about yourself. Just like you had formed these ideas, beliefs, and narratives at a time when you were nothing more than a sponge, looking for ways to survive in this world, you have spent all these years nurturing the belief that you are not good enough, not worthy, and do not deserve to be loved, appreciated, understood, or valued. Changing the very core of who you are is a long and unending process filled with challenging moments that require you to confront that part of yourself which has grown up believing these falsehoods—the part that struggled to make sense of that vacuum, whose needs were unmet. This inner child within you yearns to be accepted just the way it is.

Finding love within includes opening the door to see your inner child still holding on to those narratives. This journey is about healing your inner child who has grown up

with wounds from a lack of attention, understanding, appreciation, love, and care. This lack infiltrated your confidence and created a vacuum filled with the idea of 'I am not getting what I need because I am not good enough.' Healing those wounds requires you to first understand that these versions of you had to form this idea because it was the only way to feel safe and maintain control over yourself and the environment around you. Had your subconscious not done so, other ideas of 'No one cares about me,' 'The world is a bad place,' or 'People are selfish' would have been scarier and more provoking. As we turned into adults, these vulnerable parts got stuck in time and continued to create many such dysfunctional narratives just to help us survive.

They are dysfunctional because they do not add value to your life. They helped you survive in the best way possible as a child, but not anymore. Now, the more you engage in these patterns, the worse you feel. Even if you create a narrative about yourself at a later stage in life, it will also originate from your primary need to protect yourself. Therefore, certain self-limiting beliefs exist that eventually lose their value and effect on your life. They no longer serve any purpose except for stopping you from connecting with yourself. Beyond this is the need to recover from these patterns, otherwise you will continue to operate from the fears and insecurities that you picked up as a child—or at any point in your life. The emotional burden you carry will only become heavier until you eventually succumb to it.

This defence-mechanism-originated vacuum continues to show up even in our adult lives in various forms.

### *Difficulty Connecting with Others*

When our emotional life is insufficiently developed, our mindset and skillset to form connections with others experience gaps. These gaps make it difficult for individuals to step out of their comfort zones, creating a looming sense of uncertainty and a feeling of being left out. You feel that you are on the outside looking in, hoping, and wishing for someone to see you and make you a part of their world because you are not able to step in to form connections on your own.

### *Feelings of Insecurity and Uncertainty*

You grow up feeling uncertain and insecure about everything. You worry if you are doing the right thing, if people will perceive you well, and doubt if you can do things properly. Would people still love and accept you? All these insecurities keep you tightly wound and prevent you from genuinely enjoying life and making choices that make you feel good.

### *Feeling Inadequate and Incapable*

You constantly feel that you lack something or the other, which hinders your ability to show up for yourself, take risks, and move forward in life. Any past or present setbacks serve as a reminder of your inadequacy and throw you into a spiral of difficult thoughts and emotions that further aggravate these feelings. Thus, keeping you in your comfort zone even when it is no longer comfortable.

### *Desire to Please Others*

It makes you want to avoid anything that may upset people around you. There is a need to be nice and likeable so that you can be in everyone's good books. You start fearing any kind of criticism, which, in turn, makes it difficult for you to ask for help because you fear how the other person would perceive you. You do not want to come across as incompetent, so you do not ask for support even when you need it.

### *Indecisiveness*

Professional and personal lives are two sides of the same coin. While you may struggle to reach out, take initiative, and make decisions professionally, your personal life can be sufficiently all right, and vice versa. Irrespective of the two, making independent decisions involves the ability to take risks and bear certain consequences, such as upsetting people or facing disagreements that directly conflict with your desire to please everyone, be a good person, and maintain peace.

### *Personalisation*

You may find yourself to be more sensitive towards others' opinions. You may get easily hurt by critical remarks or harmless jokes, and it may raise your insecurity about not being adequate, competent, or liked. In situations of disagreement or conflict, you may end up feeling disappointed and disheartened even if you know you are in the right. You will refrain from standing up for yourself because you fear upsetting or hurting others even if it costs your peace.

### *Feeling Unloved*

You constantly grapple with the thought of whether you are loved. When someone expresses their love towards you, it makes you wonder if they truly mean it or harbour a selfish motive. Not only do you struggle to receive love but also to give it to others. The lack of care and attention in your formative years makes you insecure about receiving and giving love as an adult.

### *Intense feelings of Guilt and Shame*

When you are constantly grappling with the thought of 'I am not okay' and your emotional experience does not get the validation it needed while growing up, feelings of guilt and shame gradually settle in your psyche. The understanding about yourself that something is fundamentally wrong or flawed may suffocate you. If you come from a background where you were reprimanded as a child, it is likely that your sense of self took a hit. Since you were helpless as a child and did not know what to do with your emotions, you suppressed them. However, emotions do not go anywhere; they just keep coming up every so often, reminding you of how you are not okay.

## Gripped By Existential Fears

The vacuum that exists within us often becomes a breeding ground for deeper existential fears that inhibit our ability to lead a full life. We find ourselves grappling with these fears as we progress through life.

### *Fear of Abandonment*

Most of us have had some or other experience of being abandoned, whether at home, with friends, or in relationships. Sometimes this fear of being abandoned is not physical but an emotional one, which we experience when our emotions are not given the required attention. This fear leads us to become extra cautious in our relationships and build massive walls that are difficult to break down. This can also lead to excessive control within relationships. On one hand, you may lose sight of whether the relationship is truly beneficial for you. On the other hand, you unintentionally begin to suffocate the people in your life. In either case, this fear prevents you from fully recognising and understanding your own emotions as well as the emotions of others.

### *Fear of Rejection*

It stems from not being accepted for who you are by someone significant in your life. When you are not accepted or liked for who you are during your formative years, it can be extremely challenging to process these difficult thoughts and feelings. Thus, creating and reinforcing the narrative of not being good enough to belong anywhere. Since we are all social animals with an innate need to belong, such instances often leave a long-lasting scar on our identity, making it difficult for us to step out of our comfort zone, take risks, and show up as ourselves.

### *Fear of Loneliness*

Loneliness is frightening for a child. Just like abandonment, you do not have to be physically left alone to feel lonely. In fact, being surrounded by people who are unable to hold you in your vulnerable moments and validate you can make you feel lonely. Once you have experienced this emotional loneliness, it becomes difficult not to try and shelter yourself from this painful experience.

Thus, in a bid to survive and keep yourself safe, you end up engaging in protective habits and behaviours that keep you focused on giving what the world needs from you so that you can get a bit of what you want in return. At the root of all these habits, insecurities, and fears lies the belief that defines your core—the one that screams 'I am not good enough' and 'I am not worthy.' Gradually, these beliefs start to function as self-fulfilling prophecies. Typically, this is how the 'I am not good enough' cycle plays out:

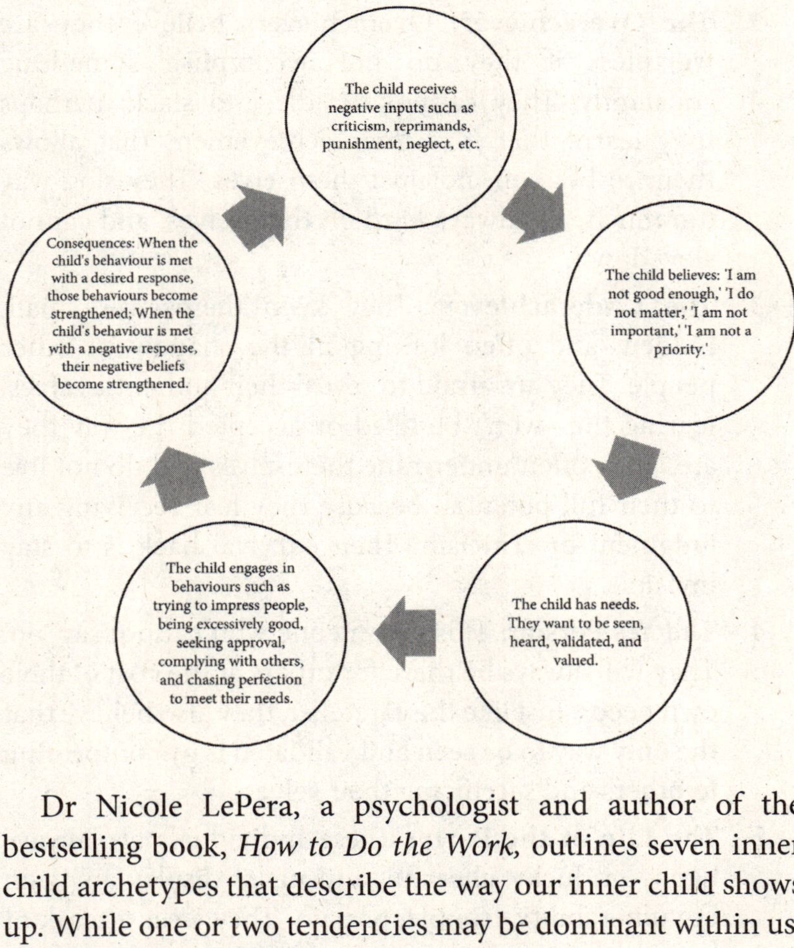


Dr Nicole LePera, a psychologist and author of the bestselling book, *How to Do the Work,* outlines seven inner child archetypes that describe the way our inner child shows up. While one or two tendencies may be dominant within us, we can be a combination of all:

1. **The Caretaker:** Caretakers are people who learn to make their presence felt by being available to others. They believe that they are valuable only if they have something to show for it. They try to become good, patient, quiet, and understanding to receive acceptance and validation. They sacrifice their needs, hoping for someone to acknowledge them.
2. **The Overachiever:** Overachievers believe they are worthless if they do not accomplish something constantly. They cannot sit idle and slack; perhaps they learnt that it is their achievement that allows them to be seen, not just themselves. They slog way too much, are always hard on themselves, and cannot slow down.
3. **The Underachiever:** They keep themselves small, hidden, and often lurking in the shadow of other people. They are afraid to reveal their authentic selves, fearing they won't be liked or accepted the way they are. They often undermine themselves and do not live to their full potential because they fear receiving any judgment or criticism. Their survival hack is to stay invisible.
4. **The Yes Person:** This is someone who cannot say 'no'. They will always be there for others at the cost of their own needs. Just like the caretaker, they also believe that the only way to be seen and validated is by conforming to others and sacrificing their selves.
5. **The Life of the Party:** These individuals are always happy-go-lucky, cheerful, and never display any sign of vulnerability, trouble, or pain. They wear a mask of being the most fun, funny, and entertaining person.

It is highly likely that they were discouraged from their emotional experiences, leading them to become disconnected from their inner world. Just the thought of feeling their emotions is overwhelming for them; hence, they wear the shield of humour and fake happiness.

6. **The Hero-Worshipper:** These individuals need to look up to or follow someone to have their needs met, often by complying, sacrificing their own needs, and fully investing in the other person.

There are also other radical archetypes you might relate to:

1. **The Perfectionist:** Perfectionists have an active inner critic who does not stop talking, making them deeply afraid of any kind of imperfections or mistakes. They berate themselves for not doing enough—frankly, nothing is ever enough. They want everything to be the best and of the highest quality, they work relentlessly until things are top-notch, and they fear being out of control and powerless. Thus, they want everything to be 'perfect'. They, perhaps, grew up in chaotic conditions and the only way they could make sense of things and feel safe was by controlling their external world. Perfectionists find it hard to slow down, take breaks, and cut themselves slack.
2. **The Peacemaker:** Peacemakers will do anything to keep harmony, as they want to avoid conflicts at all costs. They want comfort, convenience, and peace, and to achieve this, they often disconnect from their feelings. While it keeps them safe, it also makes them

passive observers of their own lives. Perhaps they grew up in a conflicted, chaotic environment that made them feel afraid and powerless, forcing them to learn that avoidance and ignorance are key. They learn to create peace for themselves by shutting down their self-expression.

3. **The Rebel:** The rebels learn to ride the tide instead of waiting for it to settle down. They become independent, self-reliant, and authoritative, and suppress their vulnerabilities to feel in control. They pave their way by being 'strong' and 'pushing through' without depending on anyone because they never had anyone. They must have their own back, and, in that process, they learn to suppress their emotions.
4. **The Enthusiast:** They are the ones who go about life feeling happy, excited, and engaged all the time. They find solace in external stimulation by drowning the voice of their emotions in lights, noises, and glitter. At the slightest discomfort, they want something to numb the pain so that they can feel happy again. They move from one experience to another without savouring anything. At the core, they feel disconnected from their self and relationships. They, perhaps, learnt to meet their needs through external stimulation because no one was present for them. At times, they are gripped by a deep sense of unrest that only some kind of stimulation can ease out. Hence, they keep running.

It is crucial to understand that whatever change we are talking about, is all in the service of affirming, understanding, and supporting our inner child. We need to accept that we all have an inner child who has the capability of taking over our adult lives and relationships. It shows up every time we engage in the aforementioned protective behaviours and end up feeling sad, uncomfortable, unhappy, and questioning our worth.

To be able to have a healthy and loving relationship with yourself as an adult, you first need to acknowledge and accept the presence of this inner child and allow it to heal. It also involves understanding that you are still carrying the burden of your unmet needs and it is up to you to change the way you connect with yourself. You cannot change the past, but you can understand that you have the power to choose another way of being.

### *Exercise #8: Letter to Your Inner Child*

If your inner child is a part of you as an adult today, then is it not up to you to support yourself?

To begin with, take some time to ponder on the given questions, which will get you in touch with your inner child and help it to develop a new support system:

1. Which personality archetype(s) do you resonate with the most and why?

______________________________

______________________________

______________________________

2. What are the disadvantages of being this way?

______________________________

______________________________

______________________________

3. When you finally decide to let go of these personas, who would you rather be?

______________________________

______________________________

______________________________

Excellent work! Now, write a letter to your inner child. Ask yourself, what are some things that you would like to tell that part or parts of you who grew up believing they are not good enough? How can you affirm them? Take the lead as the adult of your own life.

# 7
# TRANSCENDING THE 'I AM UNWORTHY' NARRATIVE

*'You alone are enough. You have nothing to prove to anybody.'*

**—Maya Angelou**

## 7.1

## Embracing Transformation: From Resistance to Change

How do you change something that you have believed in for a long time? Well, you do not change it. Often, it is not about fighting the old but building the new. You will be able to see that only if you pay attention, harness the power of your awareness, and release any resistance you face in shifting your current self-limiting and dysfunctional beliefs.

This resistance can arise in the following ways:

Oh well, it is not for me!

I cannot do it.

This stuff is good to read about, but I cannot implement it.

This won't work!

Changing one idea about myself won't create anything significant in my life!

Why should I change? Those people should change! They need help, I do not.

You are likely to dismiss any desire or attempt to try and create change in your life even if it is a single thought, but do not worry as it is completely normal. Our beliefs form the core of who we are and allow us to run our world in a certain way. Somewhere deep within we are aware that changing these ideas and behaviours requires time and effort; thus, it is only natural to want to stay in our comfort zone. Perhaps, the biggest resistance to change is the fear of rejection upon showing our authentic selves to the world. But is being safe in our comfort zone enough? What is the point of coming back to ourselves feeling drained and unhappy?

What needs to be understood is that the belief of, 'I am not good enough and unworthy,' is stopping us from exploring our potential and keeping us captive in the same story.

This reinforces the vacuum as we see that whatever we are running after is not genuine. We are either not able to completely connect with people or they are not truly aligned with our real selves. Regardless of what we do, we will not be able to lead a full life with these self-defeating ideas as we will always feel incomplete. The only way to fill the gap and place the missing piece is through self-love.

It is a process that would require you to slowly start laying certain foundations. Along with understanding a few concepts, loving yourself is also about changing the way you show up for yourself both internally and externally. Here are some essential steps that you will need to start doing for yourself.

### *Exercise #9: Change Your Story*

Write down the answer to this question: 'What will I be able to achieve if I believe I am good enough and capable of more?'

**#1: Process the Past and Pave the Way for the Future**

We have this tendency to hold onto the past where we either replay conversations in our heads or overthink all the negative things that happened to us. We use these as a guide for both the present and the future. However, it becomes a problem when we view everything through the lens of the past, which leads us to become a storehouse of anger, hurt, resentment, blame, and sadness.

To reclaim our story, we need to free ourselves from the grip of the past. However, this doesn't mean that we need to move on or forget what has happened; it is not easy to simply get over traumatic incidents. Most of us get stuck and create more dysfunctional patterns when we force ourselves to move on.

Reprocessing the past is about understanding that:

a. You cannot change past events.
b. Every experience in your life leaves an impact, a residue. For instance, a fight with your parents will make you angry or upset.
c. Emotional residue needs to be processed for it to be released from your mind.

Thus, moving on or letting go is about freeing yourself from the grip of intense and difficult emotions that you carry in your tender heart. It involves looking at the same experience with the perspective of curiosity so that you find the missing pieces and fit them accordingly to complete the puzzle. Lastly, it is about honouring your emotions instead of dismissing them.

Me: 'Ketan, I can see your eyes tearing up a bit and you look uncomfortable. Are you all right?'

Ketan: 'I am not sure what am feeling right now. This conversation has made me realise that I don't express myself. Somewhere, I am afraid that no one will listen to me or understand me because I have never been given that kind of importance. It is quite overwhelming for me.'

Me: 'I understand that this is a bit much for you.'

Ketan: 'Yes, and I feel angry! I don't know why.'

Me: 'Angry at?'

Ketan: 'My parents, friends, and some random teachers who kept yelling at me all the time. But it is all senseless!'

Me: 'What makes you say so?'

Ketan: 'Because it is all in the past. I cannot do anything about it now, can I? I don't see the logic behind this anger. It feels so stupid!'

Me: 'But what if it isn't stupid and only natural?'

Ketan: 'How?'

Me: 'These events may have happened in the past, but you are still carrying the residue within you. When you experience such emotional outbursts at odd times, it is your pent-up anger. Haven't you been holding onto this anger for such a long time and only acknowledged it now?'

Ketan: 'Yeah, so, you mean it is okay to feel this way out of the blue?'

Me: 'Yes, it is.'

That day Ketan left the session with a heavy heart. He felt low for the next few days as well. In the subsequent sessions, we talked more about his parents and childhood events, and gradually he understood that his parents never intended to hurt him. His parents had an unhealthy relationship and would fight a lot, inadvertently taking out their frustrations on Ketan and his sister. Belonging to a background of conflict, Ketan's ability to express himself was gripped by multiple fears. It took him time to acknowledge that there was nothing wrong with him and that it was natural for him to feel anger. However, it was important for him to also understand that things were different now and, at some point, he must stop operating from those ideas his mind had created at a tender age. His emotional freedom was now in his hands.

This is how it is for each one of us; this is what being an adult means. It is about taking ownership of your life and making choices that serve you well.

Often, people end up doing or saying things to us without the awareness and understanding its impact. At times, people do and say hurtful things with the intent of hurting us. However, in both cases, it is up to us to acknowledge our emotional damage and do what we need to heal so that we do not end up hurting others. Thus, when we think about our past and experience a surge of emotions, it is best to openly express them.

Letting out and lashing out are two different concepts, and most of us lash out by yelling, shouting, blaming, and fighting with people in a bid to express our hurt. While it provides us with a temporary release, it does not ameliorate the situation, ruining relationships even further. Whereas letting out allows us to channel our emotions with respect for both ourselves and others. It does not hold someone else responsible, rather it helps them take accountability for what we feel. Letting out is about understanding that our pain and emotions are valid, and we need to hold space for them. Letting go of the emotional baggage sets us free, making space for new perspectives. To be able to do that, we first need to have a vision for the future as it will provide us with the much-needed push to be free from the past.

### *Exercise #10: Past, Present and Future*

When you think of your past, what are some of the strong emotions that you experience?

- When I think about ______

  I feel ______

i. The person/people that I am most angry/upset/hurt with are ______

ii. Since I cannot go back to the past and change anything, I still want to tell myself that ______

iii. In a year from now, what kind of life do I see myself living?

______

### *#2: Befriend Your Critical Voice*

Me: 'So, Vidhu, how was your week?'

Vidhu: 'It was bad! One of the worst weeks I have had in a long time!'

Me: 'Oh . . . did something happen?'

Vidhu: 'Umm . . . yes and no.'

Me: 'Okay, go on.'

Vidhu: 'Remember I told you how my manager has been making my life miserable? Well, he did the same last week as well. I was on the field for two days, doing my work and sending updates on time. I believe I did a good job, but he still managed to find something to complain about, which made me livid! I was quite anxious the first day he complained and found faults in my work. I then became highly critical of my work and was scrutinising everything. I could hear a voice in my head that was telling me I would never be able to do a good job. But I let this voice run in the background and continued to work. By the second day, I was comfortable to an extent; I focused on doing my job well despite the voice. When I sent my manager the final report, I was prepared for criticism. And I was right! But this time I did not get perturbed by his comments, and frankly, I did not even take him seriously. It dawned on me that he behaves like this with everyone.'

Me: 'Well, that is an achievement. Don't you think so?'

Vidhu: 'Oh, yes! A few weeks ago, I would have spiralled, however, this time I could feel a shift within me.'

Me: 'And what is that?'

Vidhu: 'I think it had something to do with our conversation last time where we talked about the critical voice in my mind. It keeps telling me that I am incapable and is always bringing up worst-case scenarios. The more I try to run away from it, the stronger it gets. So, perhaps, if I learn to treat it as a friend who shows up to protect me, I can manage it better. This time, I did exactly that and did not give in to this inner dialogue. It was present but I chose not to spend my time fighting it. I do feel uncomfortable when this voice starts its monologue, but I suppose it will get better with time, right?'

Let us admit, that all of us have experienced this inner critic that crops up occasionally to remind us of the hundred things we are not good at and cannot do, along with creating the worst-case scenarios.

This voice has two purposes:

i. To remind us that we are not good enough and must constantly push ourselves to do more.
ii. To highlight everything that can go wrong so that we can prevent those bad outcomes.

Through this, it tries to help us move past the barrier of not being enough. But does it truly serve us? Unfortunately, what it does not realise is how the constant nagging and putting us down in our own space takes away our power to do anything constructive, making us feel sad, anxious, and angry at ourselves.

However, things can change if we understand a few things about this inner critic:

i. Its purpose is to solve problems.
ii. It wants to protect us.
iii. Instead of pushing it away, make room for it.

The question is, how to do that? Here are some ways you can learn to handle your inner critic better:

a. Acknowledge the voice and its negative chatter. There is no point in questioning its existence or finding ways to push it away. For instance, whenever the voice knocks on your door, welcome it, and say, 'Oh, you are here again!' Let it run in the background and occasionally say, 'Thank you for letting me know.'
b. Understand that you cannot control your thoughts; after all, the mind's job is to think. However, once some thoughts or behaviours have made an appearance in our awareness, we can choose if want to engage or let them be.
c. While the voice runs in the background, consciously choose a constructive response to it.

This can lead to a few things:

a. You realise that you do not have to succumb to your thoughts all the time.
b. When you consciously choose to disengage from your inner critic, it eventually loses its grip on you.
c. You can train yourself to continue with your tasks while these thoughts run in the background. You can differentiate better between the thoughts that can be let go and the ones that need your attention.
d. You can always journal your thoughts or reframe the negative ones into constructive thoughts and actions.

Remember, the idea is not to fight with your thoughts but to notice them, label them, make room for them, and reframe them once you have settled.

Alongside the inner critic, is the inner voice, which stems from a sense of self-understanding, acceptance, compassion, and reason. This is the voice that knows when to validate your experience, appreciate you, and help you overcome challenges in a rational manner. The more you tune out the critical voice, the more your inner voice—which is grounded in reality—strengthens, resulting in increased self-love. Your inner voice is the one that helps you:

- Magnify your strengths
- Find ways to improve your shortcomings
- Appreciate your wins and victories, regardless of their size
- Motivate yourself in ways that make you feel good
- Make choices that assist in your growth and well-being

Do not try to fight your inner critic as it may have something valuable to offer. However, take time to build a voice that knows you are good enough. Nurturing this voice is more important than listening to the critical one for boosting self-worth.

### *Exercise #11: The Inner Critic and Inner Voice*

Use the space below to draw an image of what your inner critic looks like. Then, write down all the unhelpful things it keeps saying about you.

Now, draw an image of what your helpful and supportive inner voice looks like. Use that voice to reframe all the unhelpful phrases of the inner critic into supportive and encouraging ones.

#### #3: Build a Self-Appreciative Mindset

Me: 'So, what are some of the changes or improvements you have noticed in yourself lately?'

Karan: 'Umm . . . good or bad?'

Me: 'How about we start with the good ones and then talk about the others?'

Karan: 'I don't think I have improved at anything.'

Me: 'Really? So, in the last two months, nothing has changed? You are still the same?'

Karan: 'No, I mean, some things *have* changed, I guess.'

Me: 'Like?'

Karan: 'I have started studying a bit, something which I had trouble with earlier, and I even called up a few friends to hang out with them. If I find myself getting angry in the middle of a conversation, I can pause and say that I am uncomfortable, so let's come back to it later.'

Me: 'That sounds great! Anything else?'

Karan: 'Cannot think of anything else at the moment'

Me: 'How do you feel about these changes?'

Karan: 'I don't know. Fine, I guess?'

Me: 'Don't you think these changes are significant and you need to appreciate yourself?'

Karan: 'Not really. I don't want to sound like I am gloating. Besides, I don't even think it is a big deal.'

Me: 'Is this something that you do often?'

Karan: 'Do what?'

Me: 'Not considering your efforts and victories as significant?'

Karan (looking down): 'Maybe . . .'

Karan (after a long pause): 'You know I don't think what I do matters. All my life I have tried to do things perfectly, but it was never enough. So, even when something good happens, I don't know what to do or how to react. If I did something good, it was okay, time to move on to the next thing. I have always been like this.'

Me: 'Karan, I know that you have been in an environment where there was a lack of acceptance and appreciation for everything that you did. Perhaps that is why you never learnt to appreciate yourself. But aren't you also carrying the same thing forward by not appreciating your efforts?'

Karan: 'In a way, yes. But I don't know what else to do.'

Me: 'How about you make the present your starting point?'

Most of us do not know how to appreciate ourselves because we lack the understanding of this concept. We believe that the only way to improve ourselves is by correcting our flaws. Yes, that can be one way but not the *only* way. I am sure you are now aware of the kind of destruction constant self-criticism can cause. Improving yourself needs to stem from the fact that whatever exists right now is already good. While the scope for improvement will always be readily available, we also need to appreciate the present while working for the future. It is like appreciating the glass that is half-full instead of lamenting the glass that is half-empty.

If you truly want to appreciate yourself as an individual and strengthen the idea of being good enough, you need to:

a. Stop criticising yourself all the time, be mindful of the way you talk to yourself, and avoid labelling and judging yourself. Rephrase the negative sentences that you use for yourself on autopilot.
b. Stop comparing yourself to others—everyone has a different life story. By focusing on others, you lose track of your own life.

c. Focus on your intention.
d. Take baby steps every day and appreciate even the smallest efforts and victories. You will then gradually strengthen your inner voice that knows you are good enough, motivating you to do more things.
e. Cut yourself some slack when you falter because you will. Just like you have this innate need for someone to encourage and motivate you when something like this happens, remember to do it for yourself.
f. Compliment yourself.
g. Accept compliments gracefully without negating or dismissing them.

Self-appreciation does not mean boasting, gloating, or being vain. It is about respecting yourself as an individual and valuing your efforts and actions. We all have our unique strengths and areas that need to be worked upon, but self-appreciation is valuing what is good in us while maintaining a basic regard for ourselves in the areas that need improvement. It is the knowledge that even if the world outside cannot see your efforts, you can.

### *Exercise #12: Self-Assessment*

1. List all the things you think you are good at or consider to be your strengths.

___________________________________________
___________________________________________
___________________________________________
___________________________________________
___________________________________________
___________________________________________
___________________________________________
___________________________________________
___________________________________________
___________________________________________
___________________________________________

2. When was the last time you made a mistake or failed at something? What are some of the lessons you learnt from that situation?

___________________________________________
___________________________________________
___________________________________________
___________________________________________
___________________________________________
___________________________________________
___________________________________________
___________________________________________
___________________________________________
___________________________________________
___________________________________________

3. What are some helpful things that you can tell yourself if and when you:
   - Make a mistake:
   - Do something wrong:
   - Are struggling with something:

4. What are some of the things that you are proud of?

**#4: Accept and Love Your Body**

'I hate my body!' 'I am so fat' 'I don't like the way I look' 'I wish I was fuller, taller, darker, leaner, and fairer.' At some point, we have all stood in front of the mirror and criticised our faces and bodies endlessly. We have berated ourselves and felt immense shame for the way we look.

Our self-worth is tied to our appearance, making our body its measure. Thus, so many of us are embroiled in this quest to achieve the 'perfect' face and body, irrespective of the cost it extracts. Most of us exhaust our bodies by trying to look a certain way, one different from our natural beauty. It is because social conventions and comparison have hampered how we view ourselves. Eventually, we also start propagating the same insensitive ideologies, spreading the culture of non-acceptance of our identity and body, leading us to treat our bodies in an unhealthy manner. This conditioning makes our body nothing but a bundle of flaws, irrespective of how it looks.

Soon we reach a point where we are completely disconnected from the goodness that our body has to offer. We can have people telling us that we look amazing, our body looks great, and we will not believe a word they say. What makes it even worse is that we treat our bodies with disrespect. For instance, body weight is a huge insecurity for many of us, and no matter which side of the scale we are on, it is a problem. It is so because we consider the number on the scale as a symbol of our worth. If we are overweight, we deem ourselves less than everyone; if we are underweight, we are still not enough. It is always about fitting into a standard of perfection—a standard, that does not truly exist. Before we realise it, the problem moves from weight to us as individuals. The more we perceive our bodies negatively, the more it feeds on the idea of not being good enough.

Furthermore, it leads to several other mental, emotional, and behavioural concerns:

- Low self-esteem
- Despondency
- Lack of motivation
- Feeling helplessness
- Procrastination
- Anxiety
- Improper eating habits—restrictive dieting or overconsumption of food
- Emotional eating
- Over-exercising
- Lack of interest in one's well-being
- Lack of self-care
- Neglecting health issues
- Fear of being judged

In this quest of achieving so-called perfection, we forget that our bodies are not supposed to just 'look' beautiful; they are so much more. As Lindsay Kite wrote in her book, 'Loving your body isn't believing your body looks good. It is knowing that it is good regardless of how it looks. It isn't thinking you are beautiful. It is knowing you are more than beautiful. It is understanding that your body is an instrument for your use, not an ornament to be admired.' Your body works day and night to keep you alive and kicking. Unfortunately, many of us realise the importance of our bodies only when we face some grave issue that serves as a wake-up call.

It takes a disease or an illness to make us realise that we need to be respectful towards our bodies. Sadly, people often do not rise to the occasion, even after that wake-up call. If you want to have a better relationship with yourself, you must start treating your body well. Maybe the idea of loving your body seems far-fetched, however, we can always begin by cultivating a sense of acceptance and respect for it. Instead of focusing only on your physical appearance, you need to shift it to the various functions that your body performs, because what is the point of looking good if you cannot function well? The constant criticism, judgement, and comparison do not help you feel good about yourself.

There will never be a perfect time for you to feel the way you want to feel. You only have this moment. Your body is a reflection of you, a direct representation of how you feel about yourself. You wouldn't wake up one day and suddenly feel different; you must put in the effort to change the way you feel. Once you accept and respect your body for everything it does for you, you create the changes you want for yourself. Remember, acceptance doesn't mean being complacent or giving up; it means releasing judgment and criticism.

This amazing body of yours is your vehicle for life. Treat it well so that it can both feel and look good. After all, it works hard to keep you safe and sound, so show some love to it because it is a part of you.

### *Exercise #13: Declaration of Love for Your Body*

Read and sign this contract that will put you on the path to loving it more each day.

I declare that from today I will:

1. Accept my body in its natural shape and size. However it may look, it is mine and I will show it respect every single day.
2. Act in the highest interest of my body and make choices that will enhance its appearance and well-being because I know my body deserves to be treated well.
3. Choose the kind of foods that nourish my body and boost my overall health and well-being.
4. Engage in physical activities that will allow my body to function in an optimal manner.
5. Appreciate all the effort that my body puts in to keep me functioning optimally.
6. Listen to my body and provide it time for recovery because I know it works hard to keep me going.
7. Make changes to my body with a sense of understanding, respect, and compassion and not succumb to criticism and judgement from others.
8. Nurture my body by participating in activities that I enjoy.
9. Dress well to feel good in my skin.
10. Love my body and give it all the love and nurturing it requires.

With love,

__________________________

**#5: Embrace Emotions**

Kajal: 'I want to ask you a question.'

Me: 'Sure, go ahead.'

Kajal (looking unsure): 'Umm . . . I have a request.'

Me: 'Sure, what is it?'

Kajal: 'I don't want you to answer like a therapist. I want you to answer it as yourself.'

Me (smiling): 'Well, that depends on the question.'

Kajal: 'Haha, don't worry! It is not that personal.'

Me: 'Then, it is okay.'

Kajal: 'Do you have moments when you feel low or anxious?'

Me: 'Yes, I do.'

Kajal: 'What do you do then?'

Me: 'What do I do when I feel low?'

Kajal: 'Yes, I mean, what do you do when you don't feel good from within? How do you distract yourself or make yourself feel better?'

Me: 'Honestly, when I feel uncomfortable, troubled, or anxious, I don't distract myself or force myself to feel better.'

Kajal: 'That cannot be true! I know you are saying this because you are a therapist!'

Me (smiling): 'Absolutely not! I am saying this because, before being anything else, I am a human being. I also have challenging days and low moments; I also "lose it" at times. Just because I am a therapist, it doesn't mean that my life is perfect, or I handle everything perfectly.'

Kajal: 'Yeah, that's also true. So, what do you do when you feel uncomfortable?

Me: 'I sit with it.'

Kajal (confused): 'What does that mean?'

Me: 'It means that I do not run away from my emotions. I allow myself to feel them. I cry when I am sad or upset. I go quiet, write, or take my space. I take the time to understand what is happening within instead of finding a distraction.'

Kajal: 'So, you never turn to binge-watching or doing something else to change your mood?'

Me: 'Of course, I do. I don't want to dwell on my emotions all the time, so I do watch shows or eat ice cream to uplift my mood. However, all that comes later with awareness.'

Kajal: 'Isn't it difficult?'

Me: 'Yes, it is. But feeling your emotions is the only way out of this cycle.'

Kajal (thinking): 'Hmm, I see.'

Me: 'Why did you ask this?'

Kajal: 'You had asked me to notice what happens around the time I find myself binging on food right?'

Me: 'Yes.'

Kajal: 'I have been noticing my reactions and behaviours. I realised that every time I am stressed or irritated, I start eating.'

Me: 'I am glad you were able to pick up on that.'

Kajal: 'I also realised that I don't know what to do when feelings of unpleasantness take charge. I feel good when I eat, but now I am stuck in a cycle of facing other issues because of eating so much. I need to learn what to do with my emotions instead of eating them away!'

Me: 'Yes, that's true. Let's talk more about this.'

What a dull, drab, and boring world it would be without emotions; they make our world go round. However, it is ironic that most of us do not know how to live with them, but we certainly cannot live without them. In a world that is constantly telling us not to feel our emotions, labelling them as for the 'weak', only emotions can make us feel alive. The word 'emotion' is derived from the Latin word 'emovere', which means to stir the sentiments. Our emotions are meant to flow out of our systems and cannot be trapped because they are 'energy in motion'.

In terms of physiology, emotions are chemical reactions that take place in our brains. The hypothalamus assembles these chemicals, and once released, they travel through our brain and the pituitary gland, and into our bloodstream, mobilising us for appropriate action(s). Emotion is the two-way communication system between our mind and body. It takes nearly six seconds for an emotional chemical to travel through the body and deliver its message to a cell.

According to Portuguese neuroscientist Antonio Damasio, 'Emotions are enmeshed in the neural networks of reason. While it may be convenient to leave emotions out of it, our emotions and thoughts are always influencing each other.'

We are hardwired for emotions; however, most of us lack their awareness and understanding. While it is easy for us to stay in the 'feel-good' factor that certain emotions offer, the unpleasant ones throw us off. We are programmed to maximise pleasure and minimise pain, so we avoid the emotions that carry a strong, unpleasant emotional charge. What we fail to understand is that the mind and body are connected, and every time we suppress the expression of an emotion, it finds another way out sooner or later. This is why we must work towards building our emotional intelligence to:

- Become aware of our thoughts and emotional reactions in various situations
- Accept emotions as a part of our experience of being human
- Learn to harness the wisdom that each emotion has to offer

Without this knowledge, we will never be able to completely accept and love ourselves. When we deny ourselves the experience of the very thing that makes us human, we take away the most important form of nourishment required to evolve as human beings.

Our emotions enable us to:

1. **Adapt and Survive:** Our emotions help us adjust and make sense of our surroundings. Without the sense of what feels good or uncomfortable, we would never be able to differentiate between people, places, and situations. For instance, how would you know if someone's presence or absence makes a difference in your life if you do not feel happy when they are around and sad when they are not? Similarly, how else would you know if your boundaries are being violated?
2. **Connect with Others:** Our emotions are the only fabric that keeps us tied to others. We come closer to people when we can share moments of laughter, joy, sadness, and anger with them.
3. **Take Decisions:** Not every decision is based on logic, as we often make decisions based on how we feel. It is so because emotions contain wisdom. For example, we

make decisions based on our 'gut feeling' for which we may not have a defined rationale.

4. **Cope with Situations:** Emotions serve as an internal compass that points us in the relevant direction. For instance, when someone wrongs us, our anger tells us to respond in a way that can protect us and prevent the same from happening again.
5. **Explore the World:** We are experiencing everything through the lens of our emotions. Our likes, dislikes, wants, and desires are laden with different layers of emotions. Without being able to tap into them, we will become dull and mechanical, and everything will lack meaning.
6. **Choose a Direction:** Emotions drive actions. Depending on what we feel in a situation, we either move towards something or away from it.

We need to experience all kinds of emotions in full range to be able to live fully. We need to tune into the wisdom of our emotions instead of running away from them, which can happen only when we remove the labels of 'good', 'bad', 'negative', and 'positive' and look at them with reasons of functionality. All emotions serve a purpose, and it is our job to understand and regulate our thoughts, actions, and behaviours accordingly.

Making room for emotions and sitting compassionately with them is what allows us to connect with ourselves at a deeper level. Unfortunately, we are conditioned to negate, hide, or not express our difficult and heavy emotions. Whenever someone cries, we are quick to say, 'Don't cry!' If someone seems upset, we tell them, 'Don't feel low, what's the point?' When someone is frustrated, we ask them to let it go and move on. We end up doing the same with ourselves and look for ways and means to distract ourselves as quickly as possible, without developing any awareness of our emotional experience. We engage in activities or behaviours that provide us instant relief, such as smoking, consuming alcohol, binge-eating, or binge-watching.

We seldom pause, reflect, and ask ourselves, 'What am I feeling? Why am I feeling this way? We do not soothe ourselves with affirmations like, 'It is okay to feel what I feel.' We find it easier to run and, in that process, the emotion that is trying to come into awareness is forgotten. Then, it has no choice but to take shelter in a remote corner of our mind and stay there until it gets a chance to arise again. This keeps getting collected in our minds and bodies, and, eventually, there comes a point where we cannot hold it in, causing it to burst out in the form of anxiety, demotivation, disconnection from the self, anger, and agitation. This overload starts to interfere with our day-to-day functioning, and we are unable to focus on work or relationships. Our quality of life deteriorates because we do not allow space for an experience that is natural and essential for our survival.

When a difficult, heavy, or uncomfortable emotion shows up, we need to:

1. **Acknowledge It:** It is crucial to intentionally notice our thoughts, physical sensations, urges, and memories.
2. **Name It without Judgment:** Give a name to what you are experiencing without judging yourself or the experience. For instance, if you notice yourself feeling sad or anxious, just allow the feeling without questioning it.

3. **Validate It:** We need to tell ourselves that 'it is okay to feel the feelings' because it is all right to do so. All actions and behaviours may not be okay, but our feelings certainly are.
4. **Make Room:** Pause and give some space to that sadness or disappointment. Avoid pushing it away or making yourself feel better instantly.
5. **Pause and Reflect:** Understand what is making you feel this way and why. Only when you allow it to hang around can you move past it.
6. **Navigate It:** Once you have spent some time reflecting on your experience, you can choose to engage in meaningful actions and activities that allow you to release that emotion. You can journal your thoughts, cry them out, go for a walk, or talk to a friend to support yourself emotionally. Of course, you can binge-watch, too, given you have chosen that activity mindfully.

For many of us, our emotional experience is devoid of validation. When we are not in touch with our emotions, establishing that connection can be challenging. Making room for the difficult, troubled parts of ourselves is a vital component of self-love. So, the next time an uncomfortable emotion arises, do not run. Shift slightly, let it sit beside you and talk to you. Allow it some space; after all, your emotional experience is a part of you.

### *Exercise #14: Struggling with Emotions*

Write down the answers to these questions:

1. What are some of the emotions that you generally struggle with?

2. How do you normally cope with your emotional distress?

3. What needs to change in the way you handle your emotions?

4. What do you need to do to support yourself during your vulnerable times?

### #6: Build Conscious Relationships

*Me: 'Hi, Priya!'*

Priya (looking despondent): 'Hi . . .'

Me: 'You look exceptionally low today. What happened?'

Priya: 'I am not sure how to bring it up.'

Me: 'Why do you say that?'

Priya: 'I am afraid you will judge me.'

Me: 'Have I ever judged you before?'

Priya: 'No. Never. You are the only one with whom I am comfortable sharing my thoughts.'

Me: 'Then what gave you the idea that I will judge you?'

Priya (after a long pause): 'Actually, it is not you; it is me. I am judging myself for being so stupid!'

Me: 'Okay, do you want to talk about it?'

Priya: 'Yeah, it is about my boyfriend. A few days ago, I had gone partying with my friends, and I posted some pictures on social media. He called me up and yelled at me for doing so.'

Me: 'For posting pictures?'

Priya: 'Yes! He said I had no dressing sense, that my dress was too short, I looked fat, and I shouldn't have posted those pictures on my social media. He told me he was embarrassed. He wouldn't listen to me and made me delete the posts.'

Me: 'I cannot even imagine how terrible you must have felt.'

Priya: 'I have been crying since then. I am angry at him for treating me like this. But I am angry at myself. I shouldn't have given in; he humiliated me, and I still ended up doing what he said.'

Me: 'And what stopped you from standing up for yourself?'

Priya: 'I know I am not happy in this relationship. It has been so for a long time. However, every time I think of retorting or saying no, I get scared.'

Me: 'Scared of what'

Priya: 'That if I don't have him, then I will be alone and never find anyone else.'

Me: 'And why wouldn't you find anyone else?'

Priya: 'I don't know . . . maybe because there is nothing good about me.'

Me: 'Who told you that?'

Priya: 'Everyone! My friends and family think he is exceptionally good, and I am lucky to have him because he's so good-looking and well-settled. Sometimes, even I wonder how someone like him could like someone like me! I am nothing but ordinary.'

Me: 'Just because he is good-looking and well-settled and your friends and family like him, does that give him the right to mistreat you?

Priya (after a pause): 'No.'

Me: 'Just because you think you are ordinary, does that give someone the right to disrespect and humiliate you?'

Priya (an even longer pause): 'No.'

Me: 'Does someone have to be special or extraordinary to be in a good, healthy relationship?'

Priya: 'No.'

Me: 'Now think and tell me, in everything that you said about yourself and your relationship, are you respecting yourself?

Priya (thinking): 'No, and I can see that now. I was aware of this, but it didn't hit me until this incident. That's why I have been angry at myself for letting things reach this far. If I don't treat myself well, at some point, someone else will also disrespect me.'

Me: 'I am glad that you are angry. I think your anger is telling you something. What do you think that could be?'

Priya: 'I need to treat myself well and not tolerate such behaviours anymore.'

Do you know what relationships are supposed to feel like? Like home—warm, comfortable, and cosy. Do you not want to come home and unwind after a long, tiring day at work? You want to change into comfortable clothes, lounge around, be comfortable in your space, and be yourself. Unfortunately, for so many of us, this is not the definition of home or relationships as they can be breeding grounds for stress, conflict, and chaos. What is supposed to be a haven, can make some feel insecure about their identity.

When we enter relationships with a lack of self-love, we:

- Are disconnected from our needs and wants
- Do not know what we want our relationships to look and feel like—only chaos, conflict, and unavailability feel normal
- Crave validation and will do anything for it
- Are either passive recipients or are aggressively pursuing what we want; thus, we struggle to create harmony within relationships
- Are always insecure and afraid of being alone
- Are constantly afraid of not being good enough

The road to self-love and working towards being good enough requires us to:

- Reflect and evaluate the blueprint of relationships we have in our minds

- Get in touch with our innate needs and wants
- Create a vision for our relationships
- Be conscious about how we would like to show up for ourselves and expect others to do the same

As adults, we have the power of choice, which we must use to create the kind of life and relationships we want. Loving yourself is not about settling for anyone or anything, instead, it involves choosing the right kind of people, opportunities, and experiences. When you believe you are not good enough, you also believe that you are undeserving of anything good. However, when you value yourself, you realise that you deserve good things, including a healthy, fulfilling relationship. Therefore, it is important to be conscious of the relationships you invest yourself in.

Ponder upon these questions:

- What needs do I want my relationship to fulfil for me?
- How do I want to feel in my relationship?
- What are some things that I cannot compromise on, and what are the things I am flexible about?
- How satisfied am I in my current relationship?
- Does something need to change for my relationship to be better?

It is also imperative to understand that relationships are not mere tools of survival. If we look at them as ways to cover up our insecurities and loneliness, we will settle for whoever we lay eyes on. At that point, the quality of the relationship doesn't matter, and we end up in half-baked, unclear, and unfulfilling equations. It is crucial to rise above survival and view our relationships from the perspective of thriving.

Our relationships should:

- Uplift us
- Enhance our self-worth and self-esteem
- Support us
- Bring joy, laughter, and light
- Fulfil our needs for safety, security, trust, respect, and understanding

Most importantly, as humans, we crave to feel seen, heard, and validated for who we are. We need to be surrounded by people who accept, respect, and love us. If we do not feel seen or loved in a relationship, we need to either set boundaries or move out of such depleting equations.

To be able to thrive in relationships, we must follow these simple rules:

1. **Accept and Be Aware of Ourselves:** Before building a relationship with someone else, we need to be conscious of the one we have with ourselves. Accepting ourselves wholeheartedly is the key to a conscious relationship. We need to be aware of what kind of a person we are, our goals, values, the type of people and situations we feel aligned with, and what we are willing to compromise on and what is non-negotiable.
2. **Accept Others:** Most of us try to control or change others. However, being in a relationship requires us to understand and accept other people. There will always be something that we wouldn't find comfortable, but we can discuss our problems, give suggestions, make requests, and set boundaries. However, the responsibility for change lies with the other person.

3. **Take Ownership:** How we show up for ourselves sets the tone for others to do the same. Taking responsibility for ourselves implies that we are aware of what we bring into a relationship and what we expect from others.
4. **Be Open:** Relationships serve as wonderful learning grounds, so they should be viewed as opportunities for personal growth. Relationships bring up our difficult and unhealed parts, and we need to allow ourselves to be vulnerable and heal.
5. **Balance:** Conscious relationships require a balanced approach where both individuals are equally valued. The moment we prioritise one's needs over the other, without being mindful, it breeds contempt and resentment for everyone involved. In a healthy relationship, both parties work as a team to enhance each other's lives.
6. **Choose:** Loving ourselves means being awake to the power and possibility of choice. During our formative years, we did not have the power to choose the people and experiences around us. However, as adults we do. Other people, situations, and relationships are means of fulfilment of our needs; we are the source.

Most of us desire all types of relationships. When it comes to choosing relationships as independent adults, it is crucial to ask ourselves, 'Why do I want this relationship? Is it serving me?' rather than mindlessly getting in and out of relationships. The idea of being in a relationship is to feel safe, valued, and loved—these are the antidotes to loneliness. There is no purpose in being physically surrounded by people when we continue to feel lonely and miserable. While we cannot change or control people, we do have ourselves to fall back on. We have the power of choice; so, choose wisely.

### *Exercise #15: Reworking Relationships*

1. Think of a relationship that is working for you. List down a few factors that indicate it is a good and healthy relationship.

2. How can your relationships best meet your important needs?

3. What are some things you are not willing to compromise on?

4. How do you know that a relationship is unhealthy and there is a need to set boundaries?

**#7: Set Boundaries**

I want you to think of an object you dearly love or hold close to your heart. Now, think of ways to protect or try to keep that object safe. Some common methods we all adopt are:

- Choosing a safe space to place it
- Taking regular care
- Making sure no one else touches it
- If you lend it, you ensure to get it back
- Show it to others and talk about it with affection
- If someone makes an unpleasant remark about it, you would reprimand them

There are several other ways to care for something you love; thus, creating boundaries to keep it safe and retain its essence. Loving yourself also requires you to set such boundaries between you and the world to be emotionally, psychologically, and physically safe and to preserve your essence.

It involves knowing that you have inherent value, irrespective of whether someone sees it or not and that you need to protect yourself. It is also about balancing your identity, desires, and behaviours with those of the world to coexist. Boundaries enable you to create harmony between you and the rest of the world. To set them, you must be comfortable using a short but immensely powerful word: No. This two-letter word can transform individuals and relationships; perhaps, this is why we are taught not to use it too much. Just like the idea of self-love is surrounded by many misconceptions, so is the word 'no'.

Some general misconceptions are:

- Saying 'no' or setting boundaries is equal to being disrespectful, inconsiderate, selfish, or rude
- It will always lead to conflict
- It will show the individual saying 'no' in a bad light because they will be hurting or disappointing someone

We are often told that setting boundaries, saying 'no', or refusing to follow the norms makes us unworthy. Since we have this innate need to feel worthy, we do not want to stir the pot; so, we let things simmer under the surface, until one fine day everything spills over. It happens because when we do not learn to create distance between ourselves and the world, we allow anyone and everyone to encroach on our space. It is like leaving the doors and windows of our house open without taking any safety measures, allowing anyone to walk into our house and steal and break things or threaten us with their unwanted presence.

When you say 'no' to someone, it can cause some collateral damage—they may get upset, hurt, or disappointed—and that is okay. They have the right to their thoughts and feelings, but so do you.

Only you are responsible for how you want to show up for yourself as well as others. No one can please other people 24/7! When you please people all the time, it gradually erodes your sense of self, making you miserable and empty. In a bid to keep others happy, we allow them to take over our lives, which often leads to three things:

i. Once we comply with others and receive the validation we are looking for, we learn that this is the only way to keep people happy and feel worthy. However, it soon becomes an enormous burden on our shoulders.
ii. If we set a boundary that is not received well, it throws us off. Suddenly, we are gripped by the fear of being the villain in the story and go back to being people-pleasers.
iii. Gradually not only do we start feeling unhappy and dissatisfied from within, but also brim with anger, frustration, and deep-seated resentment for ourselves, our life, and others.

It is crucial to refrain from glorifying the idea of always doing things for others and prioritising them. To be happy, you need to assess situations and prioritise accordingly. You must understand that properly setting boundaries enables you to protect:

a. Your emotional and psychological space from people, events, and situations that can disturb your peace of mind. Say no to people or situations that make you sad, angry, frustrated, despondent. Whether you maintain distance or cut off completely, is entirely your choice.
b. Your physical space. It is important to maintain a physical distance to keep your body safe from any unpleasant or uncomfortable touch. You must move away or guide people on how to be around you.

Boundaries are also significant for self-care in the face of demands and expectations from others. If we are uncomfortable doing something or need some time off, we should be able to say it comfortably. When we set boundaries effectively, we:

- Feel relieved of any unnecessary pressure
- Prioritise better
- Are more present with ourselves and others
- Become more receptive to our own and others' viewpoints, as we have more physical, emotional, and mental bandwidth
- Enjoy life
- Experience better physical and emotional health by making time for self-care
- Respect and value ourselves by standing our ground
- Reinforce the idea that we matter, as boundaries help steer our life in the direction we desire

It is important for us to understand which relationships and people are worth investing in. The ones who genuinely love and care for us will always respect and understand our boundaries instead of making us feel awful about them. Loving ourselves involves protecting ourselves and operating from the mindset of, 'I am important, too' and 'I need to preserve my essence.'

### Tips on Setting Boundaries

To be able to set healthy boundaries, one must keep a few things in mind:

**Focus Inward**

i. Notice the types of interactions, expectations, and situations that make you uncomfortable or with which you find yourself struggling.
ii. Be observant of your thoughts and emotions in such situations.
iii. Identify the source of that discomfort.
iv. Ask yourself, 'What do I need to change to feel comfortable?'

**Align Your Actions with Your Intention**

i. You can set effective boundaries when you are mindful of the reasons.
ii. What is your intention behind saying 'no'?
iii. How do you want to feel about yourself?
iv. How would things improve once you can set that boundary?

**Start Small**

i. Avoid jumping to any big decision or action when you are learning how to set boundaries.
ii. Start saying no or take a stand with the people and situations that are least challenging. For instance, say no to an outing with a friend you trust.

**Appreciate Yourself**

i. Every time you say no, state your point and appreciate your effort to strengthen the voice that knows you are important and deserve to take your time and space.

### Acknowledge the Guilt

i. Just like your critical voice, your guilt, too, is trying to protect you from feeling unworthy.
ii. Acknowledge and let it hang around without feeding into it. Remind yourself of why boundaries are important to you.

### Maintain Respect

i. Setting boundaries is not about being aggressive; it is about being assertive. It is not a power game.

### Be Mindful

i. You cannot say no all the time just like you cannot say yes to everything. Use your judgment to decide when a boundary is needed and when you want to step out and put something or someone else first.
ii. Remember, everyone in your life contributes to it in various ways, and it is for you to decide who or what needs your time, attention, and care.

### *Exercise #16: Learning to Set Boundaries*

1. List some ways in which you are not honouring yourself in your relationships.

2. What do you need to stop doing?

3. What do you need to start doing to balance yourself with others around you?

**#8: Commit to Self-Care**

Me: Hi, Ajay!

Ajay (meekly): 'Hi.'

Me: 'Is everything okay?'

Ajay (sarcastically): 'Hah! Then I wouldn't be here, would I?'

Me: 'That's also true. So, what's going on?'

Ajay: 'Something strange.'

Me: 'I am listening.'

Ajay: 'I don't feel like doing anything the entire day. I mean to say, I *am* doing things, but I don't feel good on the inside. Every day feels like a struggle, and I don't know why.'

Me: 'For long have you felt this way?'

Ajay: 'It has been going on for a while now. I feel so done with everything.'

Me (worried): 'What do you mean you are done with everything?'

Ajay: 'Everything feels useless, and I don't want to do anything. I just want to run away to the hills or something.'

Me: 'Hmm, let's say you do run away. What would change then?'

Ajay (sighs): 'I suppose, I'll be able to breathe. I don't feel like myself anymore. I was a cheerful, happy-go-lucky kind of person who loved to play sports, have fun, and travel, but now I am just frustrated and grumpy and not happy with anything. Whenever my friends plan a meetup or my wife wishes to go on a trip, I immediately deny it.'

Me: 'And what has changed since the time you were this cheerful, happy-go-lucky person?'

Ajay (thinking): 'Nothing much except for being involved in endless duties and responsibilities. I feel a constant pressure to perform well in all areas of my life. I don't even remember how or when I took up smoking because I am stressed all the time. There have been times when I haven't slept for days because I am busy working. Sometimes, I also forget to eat. Last month, I finally got promoted, and my family was thrilled, but I didn't feel any happiness. In fact, I was terrified that I would have to deal with more work.'

Me: 'How do you feel about your response to such a significant event in your life?'

Ajay: 'It was an eye-opener. I realised that I have taken the idea of "I need to do things well" to a whole new level. I feel exhausted and sad because I cannot even enjoy this achievement that I have worked so hard for the entire year.'

Me: 'And while you were busy working hard, doing well, what did you miss?'

Ajay (thinking): 'I think I am missing from my own life. I care about everything else except myself, and I know that needs to change.'

This is not just Ajay's story, but that of most working people. Many of us are constantly running from one goal to another, chasing money, material objects, titles, labels, milestones, and validation, believing that once we have all these things, we will be happy.

As time passes, three things happen:

i. Our identity becomes confined to what we have to show for our worth. If we do not have anything significant to show, we get stuck with the feeling of incompetence, inadequacy, and unworthiness.

ii. By the time we do achieve something, we are too tired or burnt out to cherish it.

iii. Sometimes, an individual's entire life passes by without realising they were the missing piece, only to look back and lament over the precious moments they have lost.

Life has a lot to offer, but to be able to savour those fruits, we need to understand that we are the source of all creation. Our work, relationships, milestones, and health are driven by our mindset and energy. To lead a fulfilled life, we need to prioritise ourselves. When we skip taking time off from life's demands to slow down, we suffer from poor physical, mental, and emotional health, find ourselves grappling with existential crises, live a poor social life, and are more prone to resort to unhealthy habits like smoking, drinking, etc., as coping mechanisms.

To believe you are good enough, you also need to *feel* good, which means that you need to have optimum levels of energy to do more. Instead, most of us only focus on doing more without recharging our batteries, exhausting us to the bone. Thus, ensure you do things that help you recharge and feel good from within to be able to take on more with fervour and passion. Even if you do not want to do more, it is completely okay; after all, self-care is about being with yourself in ways that make you happy.

## Tips to Take Better Care of Yourself

### Strengthen and Maintain the Three Pillars of Self-Care

a. Good Nutrition: Not only do you need to eat for survival but also to nourish your mind and body. There is more than enough scientific evidence to highlight the intricate relationship between our gut and mental and physical health. Ensure that you eat nutritious food at appropriate times to fuel your mind and body; however, do not forget to indulge in your favourite junk food once in a while.

b. Optimum Sleep: Sleep is not a luxury; it is a necessity. A healthy adult needs 6–8 hours of good quality sleep to function optimally. When you sleep, your body can recover from the day's stress, but when you do not allow that to happen, you become prone to physical, mental, and emotional health issues. All your goals and ambitions may go for a toss if you lack the energy required to pull through.

c. Exercise: Our bodies are not meant for sitting around all day. It is essential to be active to perform various tasks and getting in about 30–60 minutes of exercise at least three days a week boosts mood, energy levels, and productivity while keeping away a hoard of health issues.

**Prioritise**

All of us have plenty of things to do in a day, and as much as we want to, it is not possible to do everything all at once. When we try to, we only end up feeling overwhelmed, which, in turn, makes us question our capabilities. Thus, it is essential to break down tasks into manageable units, delegate some if needed, and value your efforts. Most importantly, listen to your mind and body—if one day you need to take a rest, do so.

### Schedule Downtime

Everyone gets tired of all the running around, leaving us with limited time and energy. Just like we make sure to charge our gadgets, we, too, need to charge. Switch off for a while, put your phone away, sleep, watch something, go for a walk—do whatever your heart desires.

### Indulge Your Creativity

All work and no play makes everyone dull. Just because you are an adult swamped with roles and responsibilities, it does not mean you are not allowed to have hobbies or creative interests. Pursuing a new skill or hobby helps retreat from the clutter of daily life, clears your mind, relaxes you, and opens new ways of thinking. It is also a great way to meet new people and build connections.

### Spend Time in Nature

Life has become confined to four walls of our homes or offices, making it difficult to live in the present, which can get suffocating. Therefore, it is important to ground ourselves by connecting with nature and stepping outside whenever possible. Look at the sky, take in the sun, see the birds fly, feel the grass beneath your feet, and breathe. Being with nature not only works wonders for your mental and physical health but also provides a new perspective on things.

### Travel

Whether you travel solo or with someone, it is something you must do. Exploring new places allows you to step outside of your comfort zone and broadens your horizons, making you realise that the world has so much to offer.

**Learn Something New**

Did you know that learning something new rewires your brain and creates new brain cells? It has numerous benefits, such as aiding your personal growth and development, honing personality and social skills, improving mood and memory, and enhancing decision-making and problem-solving skills. Therefore, a big part of loving ourselves also involves focusing on individual growth.

### *Exercise #17: Self-Care Kit*

It is time to build your self-care kit. List down five ways in which you wish to be more proactive towards your mental, emotional, and physical health:

## #9: Choose Joy

Me: 'Hi, Reema. How are you feeling?'

Reema (cheerfully): 'Hi, I am good.'

Me: 'You look and sound a bit different from the last time we spoke. Has something changed?'

Reema: 'Umm, nothing has changed. Things are the way they were. My cancer has come back, and we are still exploring treatment options. I know I was devastated the last time we spoke. The news of my cancer's recurrence hit me hard, and I didn't know what to do. I was worried for myself and my family; more for them, in fact. I did not know how to handle myself or them. Now I think I have become more accepting of the situation. It is what it is, and we are doing the best we can . . . or I can.

(After a pause)

'I think I am handling it a bit better as compared to the last time. I know this type of cancer doesn't have any treatment, and we don't know if chemo will work. We are still thinking about it.'

Me: 'I don't know what to say, Reema, because what you and your family are going through is unimaginable. I know this is difficult and painful; however, I still want to know what is different this time.'

Reema: 'I remember we once discussed how you can't control external events but only your response to them. I realised I couldn't control anything in this situation, and I don't know what lies ahead. But what I do know is I only have now with myself and my family, and I don't want to spend this time feeling miserable.

'I will be miserable because of the treatment anyway, so I want to do things that make me happy. I want to spend quality time with my loved ones and enjoy life to the fullest. I have let so much of my life pass by, and I don't want to make the same mistake again. I also hope this helps my body to heal. I want to choose laughter and joy despite the pain.'

I know adulting can be challenging. Well, even being a child is not easy! Life can be painful regardless of who you are. Sometimes, awful things happen to the most wonderful people. You lose people and your dreams shatter. At times, everything looks dark and meaningless. Just like every dark cloud has a silver lining, these dark moments, too, contain silver linings.

Yes, they can often be so tiny that we either do not see them or completely disregard them. Perhaps, our quest in life is to search for the little nuggets of joy that can keep us going. Simple things like watching a child chase a butterfly in the park or playing with your pet can be the most uplifting moments of your day.

No matter what life throws at you, make sure you create tiny moments of joy that make you smile. Remind yourself that this, too, shall pass and there is more to you and your life. You need to possess courage and patience to brave the storms. Some days joy and happiness will find you in the heaviest of storms and some other days, you will have to create these moments. Steal them if you must but allow yourself to nourish your inner child by doing something occasionally that provides a ray of hope. Write, paint, sing, dance, travel—do something that is only for yourself!

Joy is the most underrated human emotion, and we seek it outside. We believe that we will be happy when something changes externally. But joy is not something to be found outside of us; it is within us. We can only experience it when we focus inwards. There is no magic or strategy to be joyous. You simply must choose joy each day. The question is, will you?

### *Exercise #18: All the Bright Things in Life*

Make a list of all the things that make you smile and feel relaxed.

These are the things that will always be around you, all you need to do is focus on them to let them add a little more sunshine to your life.

### #10: Harness the Power of Affirmations

Shreya: 'I know we have been out of touch for a while. I just wanted to catch up and discuss a few things. But first, I wanted to ask you something.'

Me: 'Yes, go ahead.'

Shreya: 'I have been practising affirmations for quite some time now. But I don't think it's working.'

Me (surprised): 'Okay. What makes you say so?'

Shreya: 'So, I read somewhere that doing affirmations boosts self-confidence, and that you can change your life with affirmations. You just have to repeat those sentences and they will transform you.'

Me: 'Where did you read this?'

Shreya: 'I suppose it was some random article I found on Google. I was frustrated with myself and my life, so I went ahead and searched "how to change my life" and this article popped up. I have been doing this for a few weeks now, but I don't feel anything.'

Me: 'Hmm, can you tell me how you do it?'

Shreya: 'I have written it down, and I repeat it before I go to sleep. Initially, it felt good, but I am not sure about it now.'

Me: 'What's the affirmation that you have chosen for yourself?'

Shreya: 'I accept myself unconditionally!'

Me: 'Interesting. That's a good one. Why did you choose this?'

Shreya: 'Because I don't like myself. I don't think there's anything good about me, and since I can't change anything about myself, I thought I might as well learn to accept myself the way I am!'

Me: 'And you think repeating this one sentence will help you accept yourself?'

Shreya: 'Isn't that the purpose of affirmations? You keep repeating them until your mind picks them up?'

Me, 'Yes, that's one part of it. But there are other components of affirmations as well. Tell me, how has your self-talk been lately?'

Shreya: 'Hah! Like it's always been. I have been so stressed lately; that I feel like I can't get anything right. I keep thinking that I am stupid, my life sucks, and I keep messing up. I keep struggling with the thought of being a failure, but I try to ignore it as much as I can by working.

Me: 'And that's why your affirmation isn't working.'

Shreya: 'Because I have all these negative thoughts about myself?'

Me: 'No. It isn't working because you repeat it just three times a day, hoping that it will magically improve everything, while your self-talk is contradictory to what you are affirming. There is no alignment between your thoughts and words.'

Shreya: 'Oh! I thought they just work on their own.'

Me: 'Not entirely. We must make sure all the wheels are aligned and then push the wagon.'

Affirmations are short, positively worded sentences that we mentally repeat to instil or reinforce certain ideas or beliefs about ourselves. We may not realise them, but we are surrounded by them all the time. Your favourite quotes are affirmations. Every thought you have about yourself or your life is an affirmation. If you wake up with the thought that today is going to be a bad day, that is what you have affirmed for yourself. Similarly, if you keep telling yourself, 'I am not capable,' 'Others are better than me,' 'Life is unfair,'

'Relationships are difficult,' 'I am unlucky,' etc., your mind will try to prove you right. Affirmations are not about fortune-telling or future-wishing; they are about manifestation. Since the human mind gravitates towards the negatives, we are mostly affirming all negative or unhelpful things within. We believe that, by constantly focusing on the wrongs, we will be able to create fundamental shifts. However, this is not how it works. Creating shifts requires us to be realistic about our abilities and work on them under the larger umbrella of being worthy.

Think of your mind as a huge, fertile garden. Every thought is a seed that either you or someone else has planted. However, the ones you choose to nourish are the ones that will grow into full-fledged trees. When we do not pay attention to what is going on in our minds, we have a garden full of weeds. Therefore, if you want your mind to be a wonderful blooming garden, you need to stop watering the weeds, pluck them out, and sow new seeds that will bloom beautifully.

One of the key psychological theories that support the efficacy of affirmations is the self-affirmation theory by Sherman and Cohen (2006). It postulates that human beings are motivated to maintain a sense of integrity and can do so by telling themselves positive things.

In an article in the *Annual Review of Psychology* titled 'The Psychology of Change: Self-Affirmation and Social Psychological Intervention', Sherman and Cohen (2014) stated that: 'People have a basic need to maintain the integrity of the self, a global sense of personal adequacy. Events that threaten self-integrity arouse stress and self-protective defenses that can hamper performance and growth. However, an intervention known as self-affirmation can curb these negative outcomes. Self-affirmation interventions typically have people write about core personal values. The interventions bring about a more expansive view of the self and its resources, weakening the implications of a threat to personal integrity.'

In the face of any threat to our identity, we are likely to look for measures that allow us to preserve our integrity. Practising self-affirmations is one such way of restoring our sense of identity and integrity, as they motivate us to have a more expansive view of ourselves.

In the same study, Sherman and Cohen outlined various effects of practising self-affirmations:

1. **Serving as a Reminder for Psychological Resources:** In the face of stress or adversity, affirmations remind us of our infinite potential. They motivate us to approach a situation from a broader perspective. For instance, if you get rejected for a job, your affirmation of, 'I attract the right kind of opportunities that are meant for me,' will help you persist and have faith instead of giving up.
2. **Acting as a Buffer against Threat:** Your affirmations shield you from challenges. In the face of any setback, they will reinforce faith in yourself.
3. **Reducing Defensiveness:** Affirmations enable you to become more grounded and accepting of yourself,

creating a sense of security within—you do not feel threatened by everyone and everything while understanding that you are good enough.

The practice of affirmations taps into the concept of neuroplasticity of the brain, which means that our brain can adapt and change. Our brain forms habits and patterns by repetition. If we want to create a new habit, we must engage in that thought or behaviour pattern, repeatedly, for the brain to pick it up and put it on autopilot. According to a 2021 study by Keller et al., it takes 59 days for a habit to become automatic. Several studies have documented the power of the brain's ability to reorganise, adapt, and change. This understanding is significant in realising that we do have the choice to be different.

If you want to feel or behave differently or create valuable changes in your life, you simply need to:

- Identify the thought or behaviour
- Evaluate whether it is working for you
- Figure out the alternative thought or behaviour you would like to engage in
- Implement it

It may take some time for the change to feel natural, but your mind and body will eventually pick it up. This is also where affirmations come in. If you want to go to the gym, you get new clothes, figure out a time, and decide that tomorrow is a good day to start. You go to the gym for a few days but soon your enthusiasm wears off—you struggle to wake up, make excuses, and skip your workouts. Your self-talk may be along these lines: 'It's so hard' or 'I can't do it' or 'It's not for me' or 'I don't know how others do it.' With this type of self-talk, you wouldn't be able to sustain a new activity for long because what you are repeating is contradictory to what you want to do. With this kind of inner chatter, you are bound to end up feeling lethargic and disinterested. Your brain picks this up and puts it into action. Hence, if you want to change, you need to affirm in the same direction and rephrase all the contradictory thoughts.

When it comes to self-love, saying 'I love myself' or 'I am good enough' a few times a day is not enough. Yes, you must practise these affirmations, but to truly witness a paradigm shift within, you must understand a few things to make them work.

In her book, *I Can Do It: How to Use Affirmations to Change Your Life,* Louise Hay writes, 'Some people say that "affirmations don't work" (which is an affirmation in itself) when what they mean is that they don't know how to use them correctly. They may say, "My prosperity is growing," but then think, "Oh, this is stupid, I know it will not work."'

Which affirmation do you think will win? Of course, the negative one is because it is part of a long-standing, habitual way of looking at life. Sometimes people will repeat their affirmations once and complain the rest of the day, taking a long time for affirmations to work. Affirmations that are complaints tend to be more effective because they are expressed with strong emotions and are repeated frequently. However, reciting affirmations alone is not enough. It is crucial to pay attention to your actions throughout the day and night for optimal results. The secret to having your affirmations work quickly and consistently is to prepare an atmosphere for them to grow because affirmations are like seeds planted in the soil. Poor soil leads to poor growth, rich soil results in abundant growth. The more you choose to think thoughts that make you feel good, the quicker the affirmations work. So, think happy thoughts, it is that simple and doable. The way you choose to think is just that—a choice. You may not realise it because you have thought this way for so long, but it is a choice.

Here are some ways to make your affirmations work:

a. Affirmations need to be stated positively and in the present. For instance, 'I am good enough,' 'I can do it,' 'I am important,' 'What is meant for me will come to me,' and 'I deserve good things.'
b. You need to practise them daily. There are various ways to do this—you can write them down, read them, meditate, stand in front of the mirror, or repeat them to yourself throughout the day.
c. Align your actions with your affirmations. For example, if you want to feel good about yourself, you need to be aware when your critical voice shows up and replace its negative voice with your affirmation at that moment. You also need to make a conscious effort to focus on all the things you can do, which will reinforce your affirmation in real-time.
d. Keep your affirmations believable and achievable. There has to be some element of faith in your affirmations. Yes, they may feel a little fake and mechanical in the beginning, but if it is something you want to work on, your mind will work for it, too.
e. If you feel they are not working or making you feel good, you need to go back to the drawing board and

assess if you are aligned with them and reflect on any other block that you may be facing.

When performed correctly, affirmations can help you to:

- Change your negative self-talk into a positive one
- Change the way you think and feel about yourself
- Enable you to move towards your goals
- Improve self-confidence
- Reduce stress levels as they give you the ability to handle yourself better in difficult times
- Feel more optimistic about outcomes
- Improve your quality of life

Remember, every thought you think is an affirmation. Whether you believe you are good enough, is also an affirmation. Therefore, take another step in the direction of self-love by affirming that 'I am ready to release what no longer serves me, and I choose to love myself each day.'

### *Exercise #19: Make Your Own Affirmations*

Here are some affirmations for you. You can pick 2–3 to begin with, and gradually add more to your list:

- I am good enough and capable of more
- I am worthy of love
- I accept and respect myself for who I am
- I am loved
- I am grateful for all that I have
- I am growing and learning new things every day
- I am open to new beginnings
- The universe takes care of me
- Whatever is meant for me will come my way
- I am ready to make changes to my wellness
- I choose to let go of what is not serving me positively
- I am in charge of my life
- I am doing the best I can in every moment
- I choose joy and abundance
- I trust myself
- I am grateful to my body for all that it does
- I am calm

# 8
# EMBRACING GRATITUDE AND FORGIVENESS

*'Let love be the foundation of your life, the ground of your being. A place of forgiveness and gratitude, delight, and awe. A ceaseless source of hope.'*

**—Stephanie Dowrick**

## 8.1

## The Transformative Power of Forgiveness

Vishal (angrily): 'I can't do this!'

Me (puzzled): 'What are you talking about?'

Vishal (still angry): 'I can't talk to my dad. He makes me so livid!'

Me: 'I understand. Things have always been difficult between you two.'

Vishal: 'And they will always be so! He is self-centred and unavailable, and he thinks he knows everything—he is always right, and I am good for nothing. My thoughts and opinions don't matter to him at all.'

Me: 'Your anger is valid. I know you have tried to get through to him, but he is the way he is . . .'

Vishal: 'Yes, and my blood boils each time I think about him or even talk to him!'

Me: 'Yet you continue to talk to him, don't you?'

Vishal (loosening up a bit): 'Yeah, I mean he is my father after all. I can't just cut ties you know.'

Me: 'I know, but I also think there is something else that makes you go back to him.'

Vishal (thinking): 'I guess, I am still waiting for him to accept me for who I am. I still feel like a five-year-old, waiting for his approval. But then he says something or does something so typical of him, which sets me off! I don't know what to do, and I am tired of feeling this way.'

Me (after a pause): 'What would you say if I told you that the answer to your question lies in what you just said?'

Vishal (puzzled): 'I would say that went over my head.'

Me (smiling): 'All right. I am going to repeat what you said and then you share your thoughts with me. Is that okay?'

Vishal (contemplating): 'Okay . . .'

Me: 'You said that you are still waiting for him to accept you the way you are. You still feel like a five-year-old waiting for his father's approval. But then your father does or says something so typical of him that it sets you off. You don't know what to do and are tired of feeling this way.'

It suddenly struck him. Vishal sat there with tears streaming down his eyes and his face buried in his palms. Once he was ready to speak, we continued the conversation.

Me: 'What came up for you, Vishal?'

Vishal: 'It just dawned on me that I am the one who is stuck. I know you have been saying this for quite a while, but it's only just sunk in for me now. This is who my dad is—he will not change. Neither of us has accepted me, and I don't know if he ever will. I am tired of trying. I guess, I need to stop. If he is a certain way, so am I. At least, I better make peace with it.'

Me: 'And what has been stopping you from accepting yourself *and* him?'

Vishal (thinking): 'You know, there was a time my dad apologised to me for everything he had done wrong, for how he treated me all these years. He was genuinely sorry, and I know that because I have never seen that man cry. But that day his eyes were moist, and he was struggling to find words.'

Me: 'And did you accept his apology?'

Vishal: 'On the face of it, yes. But not from within. Even his apology made me angry. I wasn't ready to forgive him at all.'

Me: 'And what about now?'

Vishal: 'I would say, I am about to get started.'

Forgiveness is such a heavy word—overburdened with all the baggage of our past, uncertain future, and the present. When people are unkind, unfair, or have hurt us, we are left to deal with that impact, which shows up in how we relate to ourselves, others, and the world. It fills us with a gamut of emotions, including anger, sadness, frustration, resentment, and helplessness, which makes moving on in life extremely difficult. Life then revolves around carrying this load in our minds and hearts, weighing us down.

Forgiveness is about putting down that burden and freeing yourself to move on. Unfortunately, we often let so much of our life pass us by because we are not ready to forgive others or ourselves as we cannot wrap our heads around the concept of forgiveness. Instead, we fall prey to certain misconceptions, which surround and keep us stuck in our misery.

The common misconceptions around forgiveness are:

1. **Being Okay with all the Wrongdoings:** Forgiving someone means choosing to free yourself from the impact of their actions. Whether you are okay with someone's actions will always be your choice. It is not a by-product of forgiveness as people often think it to be.
2. **Reconciling with the Person:** Resolving issues with someone who has hurt you requires conscious effort

on everyone's part. This is a personal choice—you can forgive people and still choose not to have a relationship with them.

3. **Forgetting the Wrong:** You cannot easily forget something that has happened to you as those memories will always be present. However, the extent to which they still impact you depends on how tightly you cling to them.
4. **Considered as an Act of Weakness:** Choosing to let go and forgiving someone is the most courageous thing you can ever do for yourself. Sometimes, it requires every ounce of your soul's strength, yet it also replenishes emotional power in return.
5. **It Is about the Other Person:** Forgiveness is about your healing; never about the other person. It is also not about letting them off the hook or taking away responsibility from them. Instead, it involves choosing to move ahead with your life with full awareness of each other's contribution to the situation, taking ownership on your part, and releasing yourself from the impact of their actions.
6. **It Can Happen Just like That:** I wish it were that easy, but it is not. It takes time to be able to forgive someone as it involves unveiling the complex layers that surround your experience with the person or event. It can often take an entire lifetime to forgive someone.
7. **Forgiveness Stems from Apology or Remorse:** Someone's apology doesn't mean you will forgive them automatically. At times it does not happen at all. Therefore, forgiveness takes place only when you are ready and do not require someone to say sorry.

8. **The Only Way to Heal Is to Forgive:** You cannot force yourself to heal or forgive someone, as it must come naturally to you. You can continue to heal all the parts that you are willing to work on, even if you do not forgive someone.

Refusing to forgive others or ourselves keeps us stagnant. It is like walking around with an untreated wound—you may bump into something, or someone may hurt it accidentally. You are the only one who is going to be in pain. Choosing to forgive is telling yourself: I am ready to free myself from pain, irrespective of who caused it. Forgiveness does not mean 'letting it be' or 'moving on', rather, it is examining your wound from every angle, locating where it hurts, feeling the pain, and doing what needs to be done to allow it to heal.

When you choose to take the route to forgiveness, the following things happen:

1. **Release Emotional Anguish:** Holding on to what hurt us is like grasping a piece of burning coal in your hands and expecting the other person to be burnt by it. What you feel will impact only yourself. Choosing forgiveness means letting go of the coal.
2. **Shift in Energy:** When you choose to forgive yourself as well as others, you feel relieved. It is like unloading a massive burden off your chest, which results in an emotional and physical shift of the energy towards your own good.
3. **Feelings of Empowerment:** You no longer feel like a victim or that your life is governed by someone else's actions.

4. **Adopt a Realistic Perspective:** Anger, blame, and resentment can cloud one's judgement. If left unchecked and unprocessed, they breed progressively. However, when we let go of them, we acquire more mental and emotional space to accommodate new perspectives, helping us look at ourselves, others, and life through a different lens.
5. **Boosts Growth:** Forgiveness provides you with a chance to learn from your and others' actions, making you realise that no one is perfect and holding on to grudges only leads to harm. It also helps you move on in life as a more mature and evolved person.

Does that mean you *should* or *must* forgive someone? No. You forgive when you are open and willing. At times, acknowledging and accepting that you are not ready for it is also crucial—this is a release. However, the day you are ready to forgive is the day you decide to take your power back.

***Exercise #20: Forgive to Find Peace***

1. Think of the person or people who have wronged you. Reflect on the events and instances that have contributed to your anger or bitterness towards them.

2. How have their actions impacted you?

3. What would happen if you decided to forgive them?

4. What would happen if you did not?

5. What would you like to do now?

## 8.2

## Forgiving Yourself

We all have struggles in life we try to make sense of in our own ways. Sometimes, we get them right and sometimes we do not. While we rejoice when we handle things well, we also get caught in a cycle of criticism, anger, and blame for our actions.

Loving ourselves demands that we perceive those actions and moments with compassion because if we do not, it can corrode our sense of self. Holding on to these emotions, whether for others or ourselves, harms us in more ways than we realise. It is human to err, and, throughout our lives, we will make plenty of mistakes. However, the way to learn from them is not by punishing ourselves endlessly, instead, stepping back, looking at our actions and behaviours with openness and curiosity, and learning from them. Until we can learn to do that, we will never be truly at peace.

Many are unwilling to forgive themselves as a form of self-punishment. They believe that this ensures they do not repeat the same mistakes; however, this is not how one grows. This is how one stops themselves from evolving.

When it comes to forgiving yourself, you must understand that, at any given moment, you are doing the best you can. It is only in hindsight that you realise what could have been done differently, and when that awareness comes to light, it is natural for you to be filled with anger, regret, and guilt.

However, when you hold on to it tightly, it sets off the cycle of all those habits and behaviours that you are trying to forsake. You become critical and stop seeing any good in yourself, and before you know it, your anger and blame turn into self-hatred. You get caged in your guilt, regret, and repentance. The only thought that persists is, *I wish I could do something to change things.*

You are left with an overwhelming sense of helplessness since you cannot go back in time to change things. You feel stagnant. Therefore, you must move forward with awareness, understanding, and knowledge from those errors. Perhaps, the essence of being human is making choices that enable you to grow, which is a choice you need to make. If this is something that you want for yourself, forgive yourself for the things you could not get right, receive the wisdom, and carry it forward.

Although forgiving yourself can be the hardest thing you will ever do for yourself, it is also the most courageous act of self-love.

### *Exercise #21: Forgive Thyself*

Think of something that you would like to forgive yourself for and write a letter of forgiveness to yourself. You may begin with the following:

'Today, I choose to forgive myself for . . .'
'I have learnt that . . .'
'From now on I will . . .'

## 8.3

## The Gift of Gratefulness

Me: 'I read the write-up that you had sent me about your life. Indeed, it's been quite a tumultuous journey for you.'

Kajal (smirking): 'Yeah, somebody should make a movie about it! With everything that I have gone through, I should be famous by now.'

Me (smiling): 'Who knows? It might happen one day!'

Kajal: 'Yeah . . .'

Me: 'On a serious note, I want to ask you, despite all the challenges that you have gone through, what kept you going?'

Kajal (with a heavy sigh): 'I guess, it was hope for a better tomorrow.'

Me: 'And were there other things that supported you throughout?'

Kajal (thinking): 'My sister has always had my back. I have been through hell and back, and had she not supported me, I don't know how I would have managed. She was always there to cheer me up and remind me that this, too, shall pass. She would do even the smallest things for me to make me smile, which irritated me. But when I look back, I realise that those small efforts on her part made a huge difference.'

We all have our fair share of dark clouds and storms. At times, we are battling one storm after the other. Despite everything that we go through, we need something to hold on to—we need sunshine to energise us and fill us with warmth. We desire to feel the cool wind on our faces to relax, and some nights, we need to absorb the peace of the moon.

While these natural entities will always be with us, we need someone to be our light and peace. When everything is upside-down, we need to find someone or something to have our back. The paradox of life is that pain and protective factors coexist. When life throws these gigantic challenges, it also gives us something to be thankful for. But the unfairness of life is an attention-seeker. With all the negativity, we completely overlook these glimmers of hope, which appear in the form of people, opportunities, situations, and activities that prevent us from crumbling. These are our support systems.

What we often fail to register is, in such situations, we need to harness the power of gratitude. We often undermine the presence of these seemingly small things. Whereas they are the ones that have a profound impact and help us get through challenging times.

When you are grateful for all the things that support you, the following happens:

- You reframe your negative, self-defeating thoughts into helpful ones
- Your mood changes as you become more optimistic, which enables you to disentangle yourself from negative thinking
- Your well-being improves, which, in turn, leads to reduced stress levels, better immunity, and sleep
- It helps you become calmer and more grounded
- You feel in charge of your life
- It helps you see the light in overwhelming darkness

While expressing your gratitude for everything, do not forget to thank yourself. After all, you deserve credit for all the hard work you have put in to make things happen for yourself. Philosopher and author Eckhart Tolle has said, 'Acknowledging the good that you already have in your life is the foundation for all abundance.' Thus, do not wait for the 'perfect' time to be happy. Instead, find what fills you with joy even in the face of odds and let your mind add more things to the list.

**Tips to Cultivate Gratitude**

Like all other habits, practising gratitude also requires time, consistency, and patience. The idea is to find glimmers of light amidst the daily hustle and bustle. Notice and appreciate things that are working well in your life and slowly build them up. Here are some ways you can practise being thankful for all the good in your life:

a. Start a gratitude journal and make a note of things that went well in your day or week. It is not something you must do every day; allow the process to be organic.
b. Write thank-you notes or messages for anyone who has helped you or played a significant role in your life. Let them know you are grateful!
c. Maintain a gratitude jar, as it is a simple and enjoyable way of cultivating gratitude. All you need is a jar and some decorations—begin by writing about all the things you are thankful for on pieces of paper and place them in the jar. Once the jar is full, take some time to go through all the things you have put in. You can do it alone or share this experience with a loved one.

d. Reflect by sitting in a quiet place. Close your eyes, breathe deeply, and recollect all the things you are grateful for. You can begin your reflection with the statement, 'Today, I am grateful for . . .' Allow yourself to reflect on them for 15 to 20 minutes. You can make this a daily habit or engage in it a few times each week.

e. Remember to say thank you. If you find making gratitude a part of your routine a bit challenging, ensure that you acknowledge the good things that have happened to you with a simple 'thank you'. You can say this to someone who has been a ray of hope or a helping hand. You can also simply acknowledge it within.

### *Exercise #22: Expressing Gratitude*

Take a moment to think and evaluate: What are some things that you are truly grateful for?

# 9
# COMING HOME TO YOUR AUTHENTIC SELF

*'Only the truth of who you are, if realised, will set you free.'*
**—Eckhart Tolle**

## 9.1

## The Art of Authenticity

Let me tell you something interesting about trees—there comes a time in the life of a tree when it sheds its leaves. Leaves are shed when they turn yellow and are no longer resourceful. Gradually, new leaves replace the old ones, and the tree looks lively, dense, and beautiful again. If this does not happen, the survival of the tree is at stake. Essentially, the trees conserve water and energy by shedding off their leaves to survive harsh weather conditions such as winters. They pull nutrients from the leaves, store them for later, and get rid of the leaves. If trees do not go through this process, they wouldn't have any other way of processing food.

Humans should adopt this practice from nature to ensure that we shouldn't just survive but thrive. Being your true self means being able to shed off these layers of thoughts and patterns that no longer serve you. You extract favourable aspects from them and turn them into more functional, workable thoughts and behaviours that bring you closer to your natural self. In doing so, you turn over a new leaf. However, if you do not, your survival is also at risk.

This is the difference between surviving and living. You may be able to survive with basic needs, but if you are disconnected from your true self, needs, desires, and aspirations, you are not living a fulfilling life. You start living when you take charge of your choices and feel free to be yourself. The path to live is to let go of who you think you are based on others' perceptions and embrace your ideas of who you truly are. Being authentic means:

- There are no masks or pretences
- Not begging people to like or love you
- Choosing and not settling
- Being more accepting of yourself, others, and life situations
- Not wasting time trying to change what you cannot but focusing on what you can
- Making your own decisions and being fully aware of your strengths, capabilities, resources, and limitations
- Knowing when and how to set boundaries
- Taking every setback as a learning opportunity
- Not being afraid of making mistakes
- Accepting and embracing your emotions and vulnerabilities with utmost compassion for yourself—respecting your tears and low moments as much as your happy ones
- Acknowledging you are fallible and imperfect and being okay with it
- Becoming more patient and grounded
- Recognising you can count on yourself to get through life's challenges
- Being at ease with yourself

The process of self-love does not condemn you from thinking about yourself or falling off the track; there are no labels or judgements. It is a challenging path, but what keeps you going is your self-belief and reasons to do better. Even if you fall into some old patterns, you already know how to pull yourself out. Being your true self does not mean freedom from all fears and not caring about the world. The goal is not to turn your heart into stone but to nurture it with love and care for yourself.

Everything comes at a price. Just like living a life devoid of self-love has its struggles, so does being authentic. One starts on the journey to an authentic life that feels like theirs—knowing it has its ups and downs. However, in the long run, it is all worth it.

Here are several transformations that unfold when you begin embracing your true self:

1. **Being Misunderstood:** Being authentic requires you to be natural, unfiltered, and truthful about your personality. However, remember that being authentic does not mean being rude, blunt, or inconsiderate towards others. It simply means expressing yourself while respecting everyone involved even if they do not understand you at times. During this time, people will not understand or appreciate your stand or decisions. Do not let it discourage you from your path to self-love. It is about understanding that their disagreement or dislike is not for you as an individual.
2. **Chaos and Disequilibrium:** You are the source of everything in your life, and every individual connected with you responds to how you show up in the world. For instance, when you are constantly in a people-

pleasing mode, people around you will not consider your needs. Even when they do, you will struggle to advocate for yourself. Thus, the cycle of frustration because of your unmet needs will continue. People are not used to hearing you speak up for yourself, so when you advocate for yourself, it shocks them, leading to clashes and misunderstandings. It is imperative to understand that every change brings some discomfort, and, with time, everyone adjusts to the new normal.

3. **Outgrowing Relationships:** When you break out of old patterns, your relationships shift. You evolve by leaving relationships, people, places, and situations that drag you down. Your choices and preferences also change. When you outgrow certain things, you create space for new people, perspectives, and opportunities.
4. **Valuing Time with Yourself:** When you come into your own, you want to spend more time with yourself, which makes you realise that life is better off with less drama and chaos. Thus, you become more appreciative of your own space and interests.
5. **Seeking Quality Relationships:** Contrary to popular belief, you look for relationships that align with yourself when you boost your true self. You invest in and nurture them because you recognise their importance and vice versa. You know they are the ones worth cherishing.
6. **Withdrawing from the Rat Race:** You stop running after milestones to prove your worth as being authentic helps you become cognisant of where you are in your journey. So, you take things at your own pace. You

become more mindful of what you can change or manage, being grounded in your reality.

7. **Living with Purpose:** Just because someone is asking you to do something or be a certain way, you do not easily succumb to it. You think it through before making a call, be it at work or in relationships. You start looking for things that feel fulfilling.
8. **Making Tough Calls:** Sometimes you will end up making decisions that wouldn't satisfy everyone. It may be difficult and daunting, however, if it is important for you to be certain that you can handle the consequences, you do it anyway.
9. **Acknowledging Your Weaknesses:** Being authentic also means being aware that, at times, you will not be good enough for people, situations, events, tasks, and opportunities. You will also come to realise that not being good enough for something does not mean it is a rejection of who you are.
10. **Embracing Imperfections with Compassion:** You will be comfortable with your limitations and shortcomings. Whether you choose to work on them, you will still treat yourself with respect and compassion.

Coming home to yourself means being free to express your true self in every way, attracting people, connections, and opportunities that embrace the warmth of home. Despite life's challenges, you will have the support of both yourself and other genuine people who will stand by you through it all.

Authenticity is about making choices that align with you every day. The goal is not to conform to a typical personality, but to embrace yourself wholeheartedly, imperfections and all. We are all imperfect in our own ways, and that is what makes us unique. It is time to fully embrace that uniqueness. That is how you come home to yourself.

# *10*
# ONWARD BOUND: THE JOURNEY CONTINUES

*'The journey is never ending. There's always gonna be growth, improvement, adversity; you just gotta take it all in and do what's right, continue to grow, continue to live in the moment.'*

**—Antonio Brown**

## 10.1

# Harnessing Your Inner Coach and Cheerleader

Some days, you will wake up feeling low, surrounded by a flurry of negative thoughts that threaten to sabotage your day. Your insecurities grapple you in and out of your subconscious, jumping into your awareness, and making themselves noticeable. On such days, you may feel that all the work you have put in yourself has been a waste. You may question, 'What's the point of all this if I still have to struggle with the same things repeatedly?' Such days will make you hide under your blanket and never come out. Even the simplest tasks may seem like massive mountains, too difficult to climb.

Irrespective of your current position in life, you will encounter such phases. This tug-of-war between the fears of the past and the worries of the future will make you anxious, and the present moment will pass in the blink of an eye.

Such complicated feelings arise because we are humans, and unless we reach nirvana or absolute bliss—which also takes tremendous effort—our tasks will always include balancing good days with bad ones. We must remember that on days we are struggling to find a solid ground to stand on, we must treat ourselves with kindness, patience, and compassion. Those are the days when all our hard work comes to fruition.

It is easy to love yourself when you are at your best and everything is going well; however, the key to authentic self-love is to make space for yourself when you are down, and nothing is working in your favour. How you show up for yourself at that moment matters the most. An essential part of loving yourself requires you to be aware that, at any given time, you have three entities operating inside of you, and you must tune into the appropriate one to help you out.

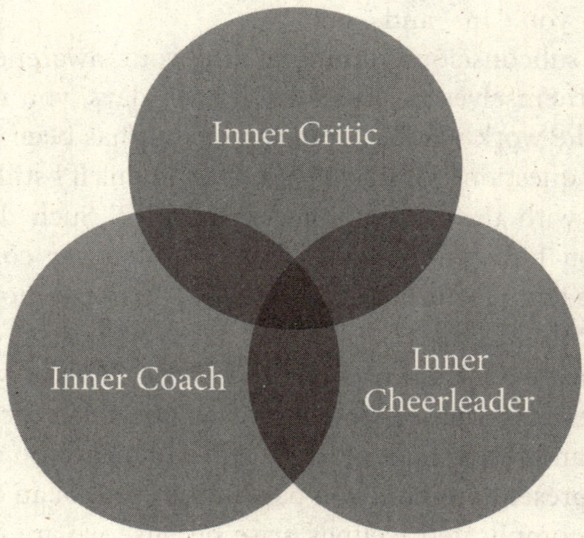


**The Inner Critic**

The small, doubtful voice in our head is the inner critic whose job is to criticise everything, sabotage the positive, pull us down, and beat us up. This critical voice can make us feel unworthy. The more we engage with this voice, the more we feel lost, defeated, and depleted. Trust me, this voice can show up even when we operate from an empowered plane. Over time, it may not be as strong as it used to be, but it can still arise to safeguard us from any situation that it believes we do not deserve.

It is then up to us to either surrender to it completely, let it get the better of us, or become aware of its presence and not indulge. We must use our judgment to determine if this criticism is destructive or constructive and act accordingly. To deal with this inner critic, we need to tune into two other parts—inner coach and cheerleader.

## The Inner Coach

The inner coach is the opposite of the inner critic as it brings in light, positivity, and balance. You can call it your wisdom guru who has learnt and grown through life's experiences. It is the result of all the hard work you have put into yourself. It is ever ready to remind you of your strengths, resources, achievements, and the fundamental fact that you are capable of handling whatever life throws your way.

Your inner coach debates with your inner critic to ensure that both can meet the same goal, which is to propel you forward while taking all the safety measures. Thus, if your inner critic tells you, *'What if you are not good enough for this project?'* your coach fights that pessimistic thought and asks you, *'But what if you are?'* When your critic claims, *'Oh, you can't do it!'* your coach says, *'Why not give it a shot?'* While your critic is busy downplaying your achievements, your coach constantly reminds you of your worth and capabilities.

Your inner coach replicates an inner compass, pointing you in the right direction by asking you the appropriate questions to influence your confidence and help you come out of stagnation. It highlights your needs, desires, and requirements and facilitates your journey by asking you:

- What do you want?
- Why is it important for you?
- What will happen if you can do it?
- What will happen if you do not do something?

Harnessing your inner coach involves creating means to strengthen the belief that 'I am good enough and capable of more.' Here are some ways you can consciously move from your inner critic to your inner coach:

1. **Acknowledge but Do Nothing:** Do nothing when your internal negative chatter takes over. Simply notice and acknowledge the feelings and thoughts building up in your mind but abstain from acting on them.
    a. Recognise that your tendency to beat yourself up is active and let it run.
    b. Avoid getting into a dialogue with your mind about trying to verify these thoughts. Do not debate, challenge, or change them.
    c. Let this radio run in the background and after several rounds, you will notice the thoughts fade in intensity and frequency.
    d. Letting them run and picking up something to do consciously creates a distance between you

and your thoughts. Think of these thoughts as an uninvited annoying guest with whom you do not wish to engage. If you acknowledge their presence, tell them you are busy and cannot entertain them. Your thoughts follow the same pattern.

e. This is not about avoiding or distracting mindlessly, but consciously choosing to create a distance while focusing on important tasks.

2. **Acknowledge and Do Something:** Your negative inner chatter is not useless each time. If there is a persistent negative thought that you are unable to pull away from, you need to pay attention to it.
   a. At times, we need to consciously talk to ourselves like a mentor, coach, or someone we look up to, to restructure this negative thought process.
   b. At other times, there could be something in the situation that we cannot manage. Thus, we need to recognise our shortcomings to change course.

3. **Make Room for Your Emotions:** Establish within yourself that all your emotions are valuable, and it is okay to feel them at all times.

4. **Recall Your Past Achievements:** Remind yourself that you waded out of the swamp earlier, especially when you did not possess enough awareness, strength, or resources. Recall such past achievements and assure yourself that you can do it again.

5. **Express Your Emotions:** Talk, write, dance, paint, and go for a run. Engage in activities that help you release the tension, ground yourself, and see the way forward.

6. **Be Grateful:** Remind yourself of all the things that have changed or improved. Being grateful for all the favourable things in your life encourages you to carry on.

While we may not be able to completely stop the thoughts from arising, we can always purposefully choose to either engage with them or let them run in the background. Bleak thoughts can cling to our conscious mind and trigger insecurities at any time and stage, and the idea is not to contradict them with: 'Oh! Why hasn't it gone yet?' Instead, say, 'Oh, it's here and it is okay.'

It has just come to protect you again and you must believe in your inner coach to talk it out.

**Inner Cheerleader**

Since childhood, our parents and/or teachers have been our primary cheerleaders; later, our friends or partners share the role. However, your consciousness also harbours a small cheerleader who constantly reminds you of your strengths and affirms, *I have got this! I can handle it, and I am doing well. It's okay. This, too, shall pass and tomorrow will be a better day.*

The cheerleader prevents us from being sucked into the whirlpool of the inner critic's negative chatter. It reminds you to be more appreciative of yourself by considering mistakes and setbacks as learning opportunities.

Together, your inner coach and cheerleader enable you to:

- Disengage from the inner critic and analyse it objectively
- Evaluate your choices and decisions for your highest well-being
- Find strength and courage to keep moving forward
- Remember that, at the end of the day, you are worthy

Thus, continuing the journey of self-love requires you to be aware and mindful of the fact that you have an inner coach and cheerleader who will always rescue you when the critic strikes. After all, being your authentic self is not a one-time affair. When you start feeling like yourself is the day your journey truly begins. All you need to do is keep walking in the direction that leads you to one place—yourself.

In her book *Magical Journey: An Apprenticeship in Contentment*, Katrina Kenison discovers this discourse, saying, 'Now I see that the journey was never meant to lead to some new and improved version of me; that it has always been about coming home to who I already am.'

# THIS IS JUST THE BEGINNING . . .

# Acknowledgements

I would like to express my deepest gratitude to all the individuals who contributed to the creation of this book. Without their support, guidance, and encouragement, this project would not have been possible. First and foremost, I want to thank my family and friends for their unwavering support, encouragement, and faith in me.

A special note of thanks to all my mentors and coaches who have been integral to my personal and professional journey—Joydev Sir, Mallika Bhatia, Sneha Shah, and Shashank Gupta—you will always be my guiding angels.

Heartfelt gratitude to Sukriti Chopra, Lisa Erickson, and Elyane Youssef for their guidance, encouragement, and feedback that has helped me grow as a writer every day.

Another person without whom this book would be incomplete is Nikhil Kapur, who left no stone unturned to ensure I had all the help I needed to make this book what it is today.

Thank you, Team Booknerds, for editing and refining my manuscript with your ideas, suggestions, and constructive feedback. This book would be incomplete without the wonderful illustrations by Yashika Luhach.

My heartfelt thanks go to the numerous experts and scholars in the field who took the time to read, review, and support my manuscript.

I would also like to extend my thanks to all the clients who chose to work with me. I am grateful to be a part of your journey. A special thanks to Dr Nandlal and his entire team at Synchrony Chiropractic & Sports Physiotherapy for keeping me functional.

Finally, a big thank you to all the readers who chose this book to be a companion in their journey of self-love.

## Advance Praise for *AI to A+*

As a seasoned content marketing professional with over six years of experience, Shah combines her deep understanding of AI with practical writing expertise to offer a resource that's as informative as it is transformative.

—*HT City, Hindustan Times*

The book has a blend of practical advice and strategic insights to help writers, marketers, and content creators.

—*Goa Times, The Times of India*

An essential resource for anyone looking to stay competitive in the fast-paced digital content space.

—Ahmedabad Mirror Digital

Her (Shanu Shah's) strategies ensure that AI-generated content remains engaging, purposeful, and true to your brand's unique voice.

—Popularreads.co

In *AI to A+*, Shanu Shah offers invaluable strategies for integrating AI into content marketing. Her expertise empowers marketers to enhance both the quality and engagement of their content, making this book essential for any professional looking to excel in the AI-driven landscape.

—Prex Poojara
VP marketing, Tesla Outsourcing Services

I believe *AI to A+* is a must-read for every modern marketer aiming to level-up their content game.

—Pooja Gandhi
Director of brand strategy, BMEG

In an era where content creation is booming and AI is at the forefront, Shanu Shah's *AI to A+* is a standout resource. The book provides comprehensive guidance and practical editing support for refining AI-generated content. By effectively bridging human input with evolving AI-assisted writing, Shah has created an invaluable tool for writers across various genres.

**—Sreeja Raman**
Journalist, translator, and author

*AI to A+* by Shanu Shah is a profound guide for anyone looking to leverage AI in content creation. Her practical insights and tips make this book a must-read for professionals eager to enhance their content with AI tools. I wish Shanu Shah continued success with this endeavour.

**—Ravi Valluri**
CEO, CERL and CEWRL

*AI to A+* is a guide that provides clear, actionable strategies that are invaluable for refining and elevating your content in today's digital landscape.

**—Nikhil Kant**
Head of brand, Even

I found Shanu Shah's *AI to A+* incredibly insightful and useful. Her practical approach to refining AI-generated content using sixteen meticulously crafted rubrics bridges the gap between technology and creativity, making it an essential resource equally for new users and experienced persons in the AI field. This book seamlessly blends the power of AI with human intelligence and creativity.

**—Dr Mihir Shah**
Advisor, GIC and GTU and CTO, Swasau Technology